THing,
A MODERN SEARCH FOR

ADVENTURE

H. Glenn Carson

Cover & Line drawings by
Leanne Carson

Published by H. Glenn Carson Enterprises, Ltd.
801 Juniper Avenue, Boulder, Colorado 80302
ISBN 0-941620-05-0

THing, A Modern Search For Adventure

Table of Contents

One of the original buildings at Sunshine, Colorado. The author found a brass nose ring for an ox   not far from the front door, and an alcohol lamp in excellent condition, and easily worth $35, beneath a ponderosa pine about a hundred feet this side of the building. This is all on private property, now owned by very nice people. Get permission before you start looking, and they will very likely remain very nice people. Four late 1800 coins have been found not too far from this location in the past year or so, two of which have ben worth two hundred dollars or more each.

WHAT MAKES THIS HOBBY TICK?

Why a sub-title like A SEARCH FOR MODERN ADVENTURE? The answer really is not too difficult.

For far too many folks the age of exploration is over. The glorious days of Cortez, Coronado, and Pizarro are long gone, and all their grand dreams. The exciting days of seeking riches in the California gold fields, vowing, "Pike's Peak or Bust!", or climbing over the man-killing Chilcoot towards the Klondike bonanzas shimmer ever-fainter through the mists of time. Even so, the spirit of adventure in all of us is not completely dead.

Nostalgia hides the dirt, the dread, and the dreariness of those great and glorious yesteryears. Nearness also blinds far too many boredom-crippled souls today to adventures never before possible in this world. Each day people actually walk over lost or hidden remnants of the past, real treasures great and small, and seldom do any of those people ever in their lives realize it. Most folks dully dream of treasures, places, and adventures in distant times and climes while ignoring such things well within their grasp.

The fraternity of treasure hunters, if that widely diverse conglomoration of seekers-after-adventure can be called a fraternity, is one group today that **knows** the truth of El Dorado. Each THer is to some degree convinced that his own personal golden fleece lies awaiting his search just beyond the next intriguing hill. That search is what makes THing compelling. Oh, finding goodies is marvelous, true enough, but THE THE SEARCH is what makes treasure seekiers leap   out of bed before the sun comes up, or sit talking to buddies around a campfire long after the sun goes down.

The finding of small treasures along the way enlivens the route for the THer and makes the big bonanza seem somewhat closer. For many searchers, in fact, the little treasures become the primary object of the search. (After all, most of us realize that while we **might** find the big one, we also **might not**). Bottles, for some, become THE reason for search. Single coins, to the coinshooter, often are ample incentives to get afield at every opportunity. Relics of yestertimes suffice to drive those creative artists who a piece at a time build an exhibit or a "junk garden" into the forgotten trash heaps and dumps across the land.

This **search** is what makes treasure hunting such a great hobby, or perhaps series of hobbies. The search gives today's TV-bored, bureaucracy-bound-and-bothered, narrowed-horizons citizen a free pass to adventure. Life becomes more worthwhile. The blood flows more freely, the mind and muscles seem to work better.

That's what makes this hobby tick! Some of us have found that the age of exploration is not over. We have found that adventure is, above all, a state of mind, and that, largely of our own making.

THing is indeed today a search for adventure. If it is escapism, so be it.

People need something to get their minds off the miserable tax situation, overpopulation, pollution, wars and rumors of wars, countless threats and annoyances upon their personal and family lives; the list could go on endlessly. THing is perhaps the greatest hobby to become a pleasant reality in years. It is one of the good things to come out of the electronic age, perhaps counteracting some of the feeling of becoming a mere data symbol within an unfeeling, uncaring computerized, increasingly regimented society. The hobby is a great release for tensions built up in the hyperactive lives all too many of us lead.

In no way can that be bad.

Treasure can be anywhere. This restaurant was given its names because the operators discovered a beautiful $20 gold piece in the flue of the old chimney when they were redecorating. It happens. It happens!

DEDICATION

I owe much to a great many people, but what can a fellow say about all that he owes his own parents? In dedicating this book to my folks I in no way repay them for the guidance and love they gave me, but perhaps it will give them the idea that I do appreciate them. That's the problem: A person cannot compensate for things like love and years of rearing freely given. It's just not like plunking down a few coins for a loaf of bread. I can only hope that what I do, and perhaps the words I write, will show what marvelous folks I have.

THE PURPOSE OF THIS BOOK

There are quite a few books of various sorts relating to the different aspects of the treasure hunting field. It is not the purpose of this book to view, review, and rehash what has already been well done. The KvM sixth edition and seventh edition are both available, and any serious THer would be wise to have both copies, for they go into all sorts of things a fellow should know if he is to be successful in this hobby field. Cubit and Lobo's TODAYS TREASURE HUNTER is another worthwhile book. A.T. Evan's has, at this writing, turned out three remarkable Treasure Hunters Yearbooks dealing with current facts and faces in the treasure hunting world.

So why another book on treasure hunting? To put it bluntly I hope this is not just another book on treasure hunting. What I am trying to do with this effort is point out a few somewhat overlooked facets important to THers, perhaps get them to thinking about the overall pleasures, perils, and possibilities of the field, and attempt to not put anybody to sleep in the process.

It is obvious to most of us who've been in this hobby for a while that many changes have come about in THing: Technological, competitive, political, legal, and other such changes are dramatic, and THers need to be aware of what has taken place and what is now taking place.

So that's what this book is: An attempt to put some THing information into a somewhat digestable form, wrap it in "literary tinfoil" so that THers may detect items of importance to themselves, and present it to seekers of treasure at a price designed to not part them from too many of their coinshooting finds. The author will be well pleased if such a rather less than magical formula produces a palatable product.

EQUIPMENT

The most important piece of equipment required for successful treasure hunting is not a metal detector. Shovel, compass, excellent library, four-wheel-drive vehicle, knapsack, and probe are fine items for a THer to have, but they are not the most essential pieces of equipment to the seeking of treasure. What is most important is an ability and willingness to use one's head. A good mind used well is the most important asset any THer has.

More real treasures have been bypassed, overlooked, ignored, and not found by well-equipped souls than ever will be known, and it is because they were not thinking.

Not that a metal detector is not a very important item. It is. Any THer should have a **good** detector. He should know his machine, and take good care of it. This is not to say he should buy the most expensive machine available. That is foolish, for there are several good machines available on the market today. This book will not go over the ins and outs of detectors, for books such as Rocky LeGaye's ELECTRONIC METAL DETECTOR HANDBOOK already has it for those of you really interested in the details. My advice, though, is to neither buy the cheapies nor the extremely expensive ones. The lesser machines often give the purchaser the feeling he bought an expensive toy, and the really expensive units usually do not do any better if as well as many far less costly machines. Find a unit you like in the $90 to $300 range. Get a demonstration, if you can, or deal with one of the reputable dealers across the country.

A good metal detector will make for an enjoyable hobby, but a poor one will sour you on the best use of leisure time to come along in many years. So think carefully before you buy.

The list of equipment a THer will need will vary with the individual and the part of the country he is in. Transportation needs, for instance might be a boat in one place, four-wheel drive in another, horseback or foot in still another, and as will be discussed, at times even an airplane or helicopter. Probing tools can range from a good screwdriver or hunting knife to a shovel, and right on through a bulldozer or backhoe, at times. Clothing can be minimal to arctic-wear, depending on the location and time of the year.

One thing is for sure. Don't buy a lot of stuff you don't need. Much you will have, a lot can be put together reasonably, and again, that greatest of tools, the thinking mind, will eliminate what is not really

A new Yukon 76 IB with a 3" gold probe being used in a mountain stream for nugget hunting. (A Compass photo)

needed. There is no need to buy a 4 wheel drive, for instance, if your old clunker will do the job. A back-country bike is fine, if you really need it, but oftentimes it is not actually needed for most THers. A good long-handled shovel, a sturdy 9 or 12 inch screwdriver, perhaps a pry bar. You see, other things may be needed on particular outings, but a lot of stuff just is not needed, most often.

If you are going to work the beaches you should have a sand scoop of some sort. You can make one, or Harry Eckert's Sooper Dooper Treasure Scooper works extremely well. If you are handy you can make one a lot cheaper out of a coffee can, some rivets or screws, a bit of electrical tape, and some ingenuity. It doesn't matter how it looks—the only question is, does it work well?

If you are going to do considerable hiking, buy a good pair of boots. Sturdy clothing and a good backpack are wise. Pity the poor guy who goes through the briars and brambles without sturdy, sensible clothing, or finds something and has nothing in which to lug it home.

There is one thing about metal detectors most serious THers should know full well. That is, if you're going after relics, caches, and artifacts, it is not just the same old thing as coinshooting. A five or six inch loop is just not as efficient for that sort of looking as a twelve inch loop. A twelve inch loop simply does not give the coverage of a 24" for those vast areas that undoubtedly conceal "goodies". Nor is there much dependable depth with the smaller loops.

If you are hunting for single coins, keep on those smaller loops. After you have finished the area to your satisfaction, however, go to a larger loop. The results can sometimes be astonishing. A 12" loop will locate items the 6" loop didn't cheep a bleep about. The 24" loop, after that, if it is a rich area, will give additional results. Unless there ain't nuthin there.

Something that happened in late 1972 proves the point very well. Wlliam Tait, Jr., of Sinking Springs, PA sent me the writeups on it. What made him sick was that he, "don't know how I or Wayne Naylor had missed this pot of silver. It was some haul!"

It seems that a Herman Rabbit had been stung once when the banks failed some forty years back, and he swore he was not going to let it happen again. So over the years he buried a half million dollars on his farm.

The money was dug up late in November by the executors of Rabbitt's $2,500,000 estate. The cash totaled $450,000 in $50 and $100 bills, and $50,000 in silver coins. It was buried in three milk cans and an oil drum.

Four bank clerks spent one full day counting the money, which was Rabbitt's "hedge against another bank crash." Rabbitt's lawyer, James A. Miller, said Rabbitt, an 81-year-old bachelor, "was a man from another era." He amassed his fortune by selling his farm property to suburban developers. Even with all his wealth he wore overalls and drove around in a beatup old pickup truck.

The oil drum, which contained fifty cent pieces and silver dollars, was so heavy that many of the coins had to be scooped out so it could be carried.

The moral to the story is clear. Caches of this sort are often not too near the surface. Large as this particular recovery was, there have been far larger ones. A SMALL LOOP WOULD NOT HAVE INDICATED THE PRESENCE OF THIS PARTICULAR CACHE. There is good reason to think that small loops may have passed fruitlessly over it.

Mentioned before, but well worth restating: Things often are in layers. Coinshooting an area is worthwhile, but that process will not locate caches or other large items DELIBERATELY buried at much depth. A large loop will oftentimes pay for itself a thousandfold.

One other thing. Make sure that loop is fully waterproof. A good beat frequency metal detector, one that is built for all purpose use, and one with shielded coils, is best for this type of hunting. It is fully functional in tall, damp weeds and grass. The Garrett Master Hunter is a good machine for such uses.

HEALTH

Health is something most people take absolutely for granted until they no longer have it. Exercise is too much like work for a good many people, and they don't have enough of it until their doctor tells them it is vital that they do so. THing happens to be one good way of getting exercise without really being too aware of it. THing gets people outdoors.

Fresh air in the lungs, far vistas sharpening the tired eyesight, natural sounds washing away the accumulated din of urban clamor and traffic, and the legs reaching out for the wonderful other side of the hill. These things alone make THing worthwhile. Just the anticipation of getting out on the coming weekend makes the old grist mill somewhat more bearable. Thinking of where you want to go, and analyzing how best to further the current quest, sharpens your wits and puts new purpose and vitality into your life. I honestly believe that a hobby such as THing can add years, and I mean fine, enjoyable ones, to a person's life.

It may be that one cannot buy health, but it seems reasonable that most persons would rather buy a $200 detector than that much medicine. Even THers get sick, but probably not as easily. They have too many exciting things to do to get sick very often, and even then they get well earlier because they have something to look forward to.

Finding an old coin is better than a dose of castor oil anytime!

PERSISTENCE

The subject of persistence in THing is something that comes up in conversations amongst THers almost every time a few of that odd breed gets together. Why? For no other reason than those who keep at it are most likely to do well, and those who are not persistent most often do not do well. Yes, many treasures are found by the sheerest accident, often by those who've never really thought of themselves as treasure hunters. Some kids find a buried jar of coins. A garbage collector happens to rip open an old sofa and out falls a wad of bills. Etc, etc. That does not mean that YOU are going to interrupt your nap for a half hour to run out and pick up a nice cache. My advice, if you think you are going to do so, is don't run up any bills on the promise of such a tidy recovery. Your creditors very likely will soon get tired of waiting for your tardy payment.

The point does not need belabored, but the best way to become a successful THer is to work at it PERSISTENTLY.

A WISE USE OF LEISURE TIME

People today have more time to do with as they wish than ever before. The 40 hour week is reality for most. Some already have a four day week, and others are due to get it. This adds up to leisure time. No pigs to slop, chickens to feed, cows to milk, and the multitude of agricultural chores faced daily by so many folks a few years ago. We have become an urban nation, for the most part, with 90% of us living on one per cent of our land.

Leisure time hangs heavy on the hands of those unfortunate souls who have nothing to do with it. What that sort of a person needs is an all-consuming hobby. Such a hobby is being discovered by increasingly more budding THers. They recognize it for the fine hobby and wonderful use of spare time that it is.

THing is a combination of many things. It is a quest, most of all, as is any good hobby. The avid THer often indulges in hiking, digging, deep knee bends, (go coinshooting and see), coin collecting, history, archaeology, ghost towning, and dozens of other fields of interest.

COINSHOOTING

Coinshooting is a splendid part of THing. Discussing it in these pages would be repetition of COINSHOOTING, HOW AND WHERE TO DO IT, and that is not necessary. The search for coins and other valuables with a metal detector is a pleasant and often profitable hobby, however, and moreover, a pastime geared to improve the search techniques of any would-be THer. Anything that sharpens the use of a person's detector makes easier the search for larger treasures, and coinshooting does just that. It stimulates thought, keeps one active, and helps a person to think about the bigger possibilities.

COINSHOOTING
How and Where to Do It

H. Glenn Carson

THing
One of the Greatest Hobbies
Today

A person does not have to be a professional treasure hunter in order to enjoy the thrills of hunting treasure. On the contrary, a vast number of advantages accrue to the person who treats treasure hunting as an avocation instead of an all consuming vocation. Perhaps, because his income does not depend upon successful recoveries, the hobbiest THer enjoys the pursuit to its fullest possible extent.

There are many fine hobbies. One sobering fact quickly found when beginning most hobbies is most avocations cost money. Sometimes they cost a great deal of money. THing is no exception. A good detector will cost up towards $100 at a minimum, and often more than twice that amount. Tools and accessories, books (after all, look what this one cost) and maps, gasoline and upkeep on the car or other means of transportation. All these things run into money.

One thing other hobbies do not too often do, however, is lead to the real possibility of finding enough money to perhaps recoup your initial outlay. Oh, true, if you get good enough at golf you might enter the PGA and make a bundle. You might buy a cheap chess set and someday beat Bobby Fischer. You might do any number such things, **if** you become good enough. The chances of your finding enough to repay your THing outfitting investment are far greater, though, and you don't have to become the "best" THer to do it.

Healthwise, moneywise, and otherwise, THing is a really tremendous hobby.

HISTORY AND TREASURE HUNTING

If you wish to be successful at treasure hunting you will, think so or not, get involved in historical materials. There are leads in those history books. There is information to be gained from historical readings that can be turned into money. Long time THers know this fact and willingly do their homework, pouring long and hard over pages and pages of often pretty dry and dusty stuff.

I have heard many would-be THers proclaim their abilities, then state their intentions of not wasting time with a lot of reading. I also have noticed they always want someone to give them a lead. Good leads just are not given away. Not often, at least. There is not much sense in laboring at intensive research, coming up with a really hot lead, rushing out, and asking somebody else to go dig it up. You cannot expect people to do that sort of work for you.

There are exceptions. Some people are researchers. A few would rather do the researching and really don't care to get afield. A few workable partnerships with a good researcher and one or more hard-working field men have been quite successful. Such is not common, however, and I would not count on anyone else doing that while you go out and gather the loot. Researching projects on your own is the only real answer.

Why read historical materials? The reasons for THers to do so are manifold. The magnitude of the possibilities of potential recoveries is too fantastic for most people to grasp in its entirety. It boils down, though, to one main concept: HISTORY IS BUT A RECORD OF WHAT LIVING PEOPLE DID. These people down through history lived, they loved, they fought against man, nature, and circumstance, they got sick, they fled in the face of danger, and they often died before they were ready. Wealth was gathered together. For protection it was well hidden. Sometimes it was lost, and often it was stolen. Riches of fairy-tale proportions still today lie unseen in vaults hidden before some of our ancestors wiped off the blood and the blue paint and accepted the Roman conquest of southern England.

Robbers looted and buried their loot. Much of it today is right where the rascals put it: Theives did not have the judicial cloak of protection they enjoy at this time in the United States, and they paid swiftly and dearly if and when they were apprehended. Executions were public and gory, making the so-called "harsh" frontier lynchings of our pioneer west seem like Sunday-school picnics.

Banking is new, and down through history anyone with money or gathered wealth of any kind was forced to devise their own banking system. Think of the plagues, the endless skirmishes, battles, and engulfing wars that swept Europe, Asia, Africa—yes, and even the Americas—for **centuries** before Christopher Columbus was even potty trained. Many people who had wealth did not live to dig it up, or even tell anyone else where it was hidden. The Black Death was perhaps the worst of many plagues sweeping at various times through Europe. Although it wiped out as much or more than fifty percent of some European cities' populations there were other seldom heard of epidemics that were terrible enough in their own rights. Wars thinned the population in a way we can today scarcely believe, as usual far harder on civilian populations that it was on the actual weilders of weapons. Famine, too, raised its boney frame all too often, and beckoned graveward with grisly claw untold starving thousands.

It is not hard to imagine, when one starts to study, the caches large and small that lie hidden all through the long-inhabited lands. Why study history? The point should already begin to be obvious from what has been mentioned, but let us to a degree get a closer perspective.

This book is primarily written for THers in North America, although I would hope that much of what is said would apply to any THer anywhere.

Therefore we will not spend much time thinking about the bitter Hellene onslaught against a decadent Persian Empire. Alexander gathered a fantastic amount of wealth during his Grecian blitzkriegg. Literal cartloads of silver abruptly passed over into the Greeks' hands. What they did not get, and what has even yet not been recovered, is the simply unbelievable hoard of Persian gold. That was carefully buried by loyal troops before the complete collapse of Persia. Most of those loyal men perished in their losing battle against the highly armored Greek phalanxes. Those that did not perish were not about to lead their enemies to such a treasure, and the secret of that wealth's location vanished.

A casual mention of Tamarlane, who built tall pyramids of the skulls of those who opposed him, and looted a short-lived empire almost as large as Alexander's, only hints of treasures still unfound. Or Ghengis Khan, whose Mongol hordes killed almost a million Persians so that, as in the merciless invader's own words, he might have more horse pasture. His Oriental horsemen ravaged through palaces and marketplaces across Asia and into Europe. Their personal bundles undoubtedly held prince's ransoms, and how many quickly hide-wrapped treasure troves were hastily buried beneath the night's bedroll and not reclaimed as the horseman vaulted into early morning battle and sudden death? A most interesting question!

14

Napoleon? How many skirmishes? How many nation-shaking battles? Can we even imagine the hideous retreat from Moscow, the gore at Waterloo, or the earlier Spanish or Italian campaigns? French bones were scattered amongst those of most other nationalities, and often as not an unclaimed cache carefully prepared against the day of returning to France even yet rests where it was hidden early in the 1800's.

The Venitians, the Geonese, the Prussians, The Poles, the Vikings. All these and many others had their glorious years. Wealth came home with the surviving warriors, and much of it was buried. Gold and silver were hard to come by, and such things were always quickly and carefully hidden away, often underground. Have you ever seen a map of the Germanic states before Napoleon consolidated them, to a degree? There must have been constant, perpetual bickerings. Those stone castles were not built just for decoration. Feudalism, after all, was simply a protective measure developed after the fall of Rome to retain at least some degree of safety against utter lawless chaos. The word, vandalism, you know, comes from the Vandal tribe, who were some pretty tough people. They took **anything** they wanted from whomever they could take it from. Wine, women, and they made up their own songs. What they could not carry off they killed, burned, or knocked down. The people who think we have it tough these days could not have read or thought much about history.

These things are interesting enough, but on to the Americas. You should know, however, we are in a few brief paragraphs casually skipping over THing possibilities totaling in the BILLIONS of dollars, **face** value. Most of us, nevertheless cannot really get too far from where we live. Most of us have not the time, capital, command of languages, or the pure guts to undertake a well-thought-out foreign venture. Few who have all these attributes have done or are willing or able to do the research. Without that, even though one has all the other attributes, he'd either better hire the research done or stay home.

Let us somewhat quickly think about a few various historical eras of THing importance in the Americas. This, after all, is not a history text. These things are mentioned primarily to get folks to develop their own areas of interest.

There is no easy way to list all the incidents, eras, and movements that undoubtedly contribute to treasure hunting opportunities. That is what the history books do. The important message here is that by deciding what interests you, you can research periods of history and come up with multitudes of detail and direction that point to THing possibilities.

The early Europeans in this country, one should remember, came to get rich and return to their homelands to live the good life. That was their purpose, Spanish, English, French, Portuguese, Dutch, Russian, or whatever. A few did just that. Some found wealth, in various forms, and their bones marked the spot where Indian, animal, natural disaster, or greedy companion abruptly ended their dreams of wealth and splendor.

Even before the coming of the Europeans, and we have to count the Viking explorations as being of considerable importance and interest in certain areas, the Indians amassed their own hordes of wealth. Then came the European exploration and colonization period. Conflicts quickly arose over who got what. The Spanish, French, English, many, many different Indian tribes, and the Russians were to squabble over the land and all its wealth for a long time. The Dutch, Germans, Swedes and a good many others lost out quite early or came too late to even get a foothold.

All of these periods and movements, early though they may be, have a great deal of written information. It is amazing what kinds of things, of real value to a THer, can be gleaned out of early documents. Real treasure leads are right there, awaiting somebody's knowing eye. Reports of skirmishes, letters talking about a sudden Indian raid and which **wealthy** family was slain, man, woman, and children, old journals, and on and on.

There were all sorts of colonial squabbles. The French and Indian War, the Revolution, the War of 1812. Those individuals LIVED, and many DIED during those upheavals. Those of you who hunt the Civil War battle grounds know what tremendous finds can be made. Items from even earlier periods of our nation's history are still there, too, and far less publicized. Pirates were suppressed by the early U.S. Navy. Indians were exterminated or driven westward from their homelands. Frontiersmen dwelt upon the edge of the wilderness, and many of such folk perished. The United States fought Mexico, it fought Spain, and it continued its conflict with the Indians.

Transportation routes sprang up. Wagon roads, canals, seaports, stagecoach lines, the fantastic mushroom-like growth of the railroads, and the wagon trains westward all left THing opportunities galore.

Periods of inflation swept the country. Mining activities shoved sanity aside and drove men who would not know a chunk of gold from a cowpie westward. Horrid recessions and depression engulfed the nation at times like tidal waves, dragging many debtors rip-tide fashion into deep pools of grinding poverty. Promotional schemes flourished, making many a Scoundrel wealthy. Gambling was rampant, and fortunes changed hands on the turn of a card—marked, like as not. Lead ended many an argument, and any divulgance of a well-hidden cache, quite often.

The scourge of disease flailed the westering land. Diptheria, typhus, smallpox, typhoid fever, and pneumonia took thousands, often abruptly. A ruptured appendix was a death sentence. Rabies, also, and many an innocent dog was shot dead in the street because someone **thought** he looked funny, and few scolded a man for such an act.

Again, all these incidents were faithfully recorded. Newspapers, early magazines, personal letters, journals and diaries, governmental reports, and hundreds of other sources list THing opportunities in fantastic detail. True, the THer has to fill in a good many gaps, but the facts, the sites, the dates, and all sorts of information is readily available. It is astonishing, but sheer laziness has kept most of these things secrets for years.

A wise old saying indicates the best hiding place is right out in plain sight, where anyone can see it. There are many THing opportunities lurking in our libraries.

One is not going to go clear through the entire library, of course. Choose! Pick an era. Select a period, or a movement. Specialize a good deal, and read carefully all about that which most interests you. Crooks, special kinds of crooks, special kinds of crooks in certain places—preferably not too far from where you live, even if they were there before you were born. Following after today's crook, especially if a large amount of wealth is involved, can get a THer shot very dead.

Learn to spot interest tags. Some researchers like to seek out facts about recluses; interesting facts like estates surprisingly small, or death by malnutrition because of miserliness even though records indicate money. Others look for wealthy people who did not have many close friends, or for eccentricities, or for regular or frequent trips to a certain locale away from home. Things of that sort become little red arrows to one who works at researching, pointing right at areas for deeper study.

History? You'd better believe that THers must become interested and involved in historical materials. It will spell the difference between wild goose chases and money in the pocket. A good researcher does not need to go around the country chasing legendary loot that has been blown all out of proportion to reality, if it indeed ever existed at all. He develops his own leads, works only on that which seems highly possible of recovery, and leaves the wild, pie-in-the-sky, fly-by-the-seat-of-your-pants book and magazine rehashes to daydreamers and wild-goose chasers.

HISTORICAL SOCIETIES AND OTHER RESEARCH AIDS

Almost all the states have state archives and a state historical society. The records of these places are impressive, usually in rather good order, and somewhat staggering in their scope. The state historical societies are usually supported by membership fees and contributions, and because most such membership rolls are extensive and contain many people interested in and proud of their state's history, these organizations are able to compile and keep in order factual materials of all sorts. The state archives are supported by state and federal funds.

Many counties and communities have their own historical societies, some with museums, some without. A good number of such places have astonishing accumulations of artifacts, records, ledgers, diaries, and all sorts of information of possible interest and use to a THer.

It is useful to you to find out what organizations of this sort are in your state and area, and learn how to make the best use of them. A complete list would take up a book in itself, for there are several thousand historical societies around the country. Over three thousand maintain museums. This does not count historical clubs, of which there is an even larger number. You are bypassing a most helpful research tool if you don't use such organizations. Becoming a member is neither expensive nor bothersome, and doing so opens research doorways you probably didn't even know were in the wall.

There are other research aids. I hate to mention it, but the public library is too seldom used by some "THers" I know, who wonder why they don't ever run across any leads. The U.S. Government has all sorts of publications, offices, and information. Every mining state has a state mining agency directory. The U.S. Forest Service has regional offices that can answer a good many questions a THer might have, as does the bureau of land management offices scattered throughout the land. Various state and county offices have records and statistics that may be valuable for particular projects. The police department, street maintenance, the county sheriff's office: All these and many others can be of definite help. Information from the last few may or may not be easy to get.

Do a bit of thinking, and you will see collections of facts and dates available to you. Using your head, after all, is a prerequisite for becoming a successful THer.

BUILDING A LEAD FILE

How can something as simple as building a lead file cause such a great number of THers so much trouble? How can the lack of doing it be such a common weakness?

Inertia is a good answer in most cases. Laziness, lack of even a little knowledge—these reasons are roadblock enough.

You had best know, though, if you are really serious about THing that research and careful thought about what you wish to do is a must if you ever expect to be successful even a little bit. Don't expect someone else to come running over, grab you by the hand, and tell you that you must dig exactly three feet east of the big rock south of Farmer Jones' foundation, for he hid $2,000 in gold coins in a pot two feet down. Things don't happen just that way.

It is almost that simple, somethimes, if you develop the ability to put things you hear, and see, and hear together. Building up a file of such items is imperative unless you are a genius or have access to a large computer. It doesn't matter how good a memory you have, you will forget things. Even if you don't forget isolated items you probably will fail to associate associations and relations of things. People have gone around with key clues in their heads for years without attaching any importance to them, even though they are looking for the item the clue would lead them to.

All of us have special interests. That is the best way to start a lead file. Say there was an old robbery and to your knowledge the money is still cached in the area. You've thought about looking for it. Stop just thinking and start a file.

One simple method is to begin with manila folders. Clippings, your own notes, photographs, items from books, statistics from the courthouse and sheriff's office—all these can go into the folder. Notes from those who saw or heard something about the incident can be important, sketchy though such individual notes might be.

An even better system, especially if you are working on something really interesting and important, is to compile your facts on 3 by 5 cards. 3 by 5 paper slips will work, but they really are too thin. They crumple and sometimes get wadded up or torn. The cards will last through much handling, sorting, use and re-use.

Ignore the first notion to just write all your information down on sheets of paper. If you ignore this warning you will find yourself falling into several errors common to all who succumb to attempting to do things the quickest, easiest way. You will repeat yourself. You will omit important items. The first wastes time, not saves it. The second, omitting items, is most of the time the death of solving a problem.

On one series of cards jot eyewitness accounts. At the top of the card write a key word. EYEWITNESS, for example. Next to it Ace Robbery, (the name of the incident). Also Jack Smith, the name of the eyewitness. All this on the top line makes for easy access if you are thumbing through. Don't try to get everything on one card. Old Jack Smith may have to have a couple dozen cards, because he was a regular blabbermouth after that particular robbery. You may have several cards, but one little word on one of those cards might give you an insight that tells you eventually where that loot still is. Jack didn't know. He was just parroting something he heard.

The next series of cards might be for statistics on the robbery. Another group could be for opinions of where the gang went right after the robbery, before they were shot dead.

A shoebox will keep you from having 3 by 5 cards all over the house. Tape on a label that sticks up higher than the rest of the cards to divide the various groups. Photos really don't have to be on cards, but that box keeps them right there with everything else.

Keep the process simple. Simple things are the best things. You are not writing a thesis, although you may, before you are done with a given project, do an equal amount of work to what is done on some theses. You have to please nobody but yourself. Just don't do such a slipshod, lousy job that you cannot decipher your own notes. There is nothing so frustrating as to realize that something was of an unbelievable importance, but you either have it no longer or can't figure out what your scribbles meant.

This simple system allows one to quit working on a project for any length of time. Other projects can divert your attention and the facts stay right where you left them, in order. You can pick up right where you left off. This is good, oftentimes, to let something set. I have known Apache Jim, for instance, to get wall-eyed frustrated, throw everything down in disgust and walk away from a project for several weeks or several months.

Even longer, sometimes. Then, for he has thought it over and over, even when he didn't even realize he was analyzing it, he would come back at it with new ideas and fresh perspectives.

As new facts come up they too can be put on cards and sorted into place. At such times it is a wise thing to go over, quickly, what you've already accumulated. It is at such times that clues often drop into long-puzzling gaps.

This old well is a few steps east of what once was the toll house for the road leading up to the gold-producing area around Jamestown, Colorado. Who knows what kinds of caches are still within a few hundred yards of this spot.

ONE'S PERSONAL
RESEARCH LIBRARY

Many books, magazines, newspapers, pamphlets, and other such literature you will want to use in researching possible leads can be obtained in your local or a nearby city library. You will, however, probably wish to build up your own, personal library. Some books you will want to have instantly available. It is most frustrating to need a particular book, run down to the library, and discover once there that the book has been checked out by another person. Or, what is worse, just gone. If you are serious about THing you will undoubtedly build up your library.

Many good books are available to the budding THer. You will indeed need to find a cache if you desire to purchase them all. Many good books are virtually impossible to find, for many have gone out of print. New books come out, some with fascinating titles and little pertinent information. A pretty cover does not a THing book make, to paraphrase an old quote. There are a few excellent THing books overlooked because of plain dustjackets, poorly chosen titles, or other similar reasons.

It is not the author's intent to list all the possible THing books available. It would take too many pages, for one thing. Several organizations have a rather complete current book list. Each THer should study such lists carefully, selecting only the books he really wants or needs. Uselessly purchased books only divert funds that could be more wisely spent on literature of more value, and such books only take up shelf room. They are seldom read.

A THer should have a few general books. Karl von Mueller's Treasure Hunters Manual, the sixth or seventh edition, or both, are excellent choices. Both, because they are absolutely different books, supplementing instead of repeating each other. Cubit and Lobo have a good general book recently on the market, too: TODAY'S TREASURE HUNTER. There are others, and good ones, but this need not become a booklist. It certainly is no attempt to promote books or state which books are the very best.

After choosing a few good general THing books a person should look to his special interests. It is amazing how many rather comprehensive books have been written on the various facets of treasure hunting. If you are a bottle nut there are many excellent books. If you collect barbed-wire there are several really good books. There are books on insulators, fruit jars, pocket knives, clocks, old books, antiques of all kinds, and even out-houses. There are books on ghost towns. General ghost town books, regional, state, and even specific towns of major historical importance and interest. There are clues and leads galore in such volumes, if the reader uses his head and supplemental material such as maps, newspapers, and periodicals. If you have a special interest there just may be a book that can help you.

Some books are hard to get. Books of special interest are often put out in extremely limited editions, sometimes only a thousand or fewer copies. It may be a good book, and still not sell well enough to warrant the expense of reprinting. Out of print it goes, and its title drops into oblivion. If you have contact with an organization that will help you find such books it can be a great help to you. Foul Anchor Archives for years tried, and was good at it, to serve in such a way. Frontier Press has been able to often come up with hard to get titles, as has the Examimo establishment.

You should check carefully into books concerning your state or region. There have been good treasure hunting books come out on regions, states, and even localities these past few years. Increasingly so as the hobby field has grown, for people have pursued their interests and a few of those capable of writing about such things have been doing so.

Find out if you can get old newspapers or magazines, circulars, or other printed material dealing with your area in its yesteryears. Such items can have absolutely dozens of good leads. Such items in themselves make an interesting collection, too, and can have a considerable cash value.

If someone in your area has old photographs, see if you can go through them and get duplicates made. After all, you just might one day decide to put together an article, or even a small book. There often is a market for informative pictures. People who put together such collections, by the way, probably do more good for future historians than can ever be imagined, and they might make a few dollars in the process. They will if it is done right.

The author took from a dump-bound truck a cardboard box, for instance, FULL to running over of old musical records, mostly pre-1945. HMMM? The stuff thrown away in this country, that could be converted into spendable green stuff, is unbelievable.

Frequent the used book stores. They can be interesting, and often there are bargains in them good enough to cause downright amusement. It will certainly supplement your personal library. If you look long and hard enough you probably find for a fraction of their original cost books you have long desired.

THE
COUNTY
COURTHOUSE

The amount of information in any county courthouse is absolutely staggering. Such gigantic files of all sorts of vital statistics and facts have piled up that most counties have had to go to microfilm records. There was not enough room to store all that information in written form.

What's there, and why should a THer look to the county courthouse in his researching? The reasons are as diverse as the people who could use those files. Sales and purchases of properties, dates, forclosures, acreages, property lines, names of people, town plats, right-of-ways, births, deaths, notes, marriages, divorces, and all of it right there for anyone who wants to seek it out.

One can prove that a certain person lived at or at least owned a given piece of property, know exactly where that property is located, who presently owns it, where an important property line actually is, or was: pieces of land have a way of being sold off, over the years, and that old barn could now be on the neighbor's land.

If a THer is working on a project in a given town he should not hesitate to check out these basic facts. Those records will tell him if there is any use or not of continuing the project. Research does not do itself, though. Ask those people in the courthouse how to look up what you need, for they are hired to help people needing information.

Be discreet, and even use another example than the actual party in which you are actually interested. If you show too much interest in a particular situation, and there were treasure stories about that person or place, your prying could awaken interest that would, for your security's sake, best be left dormant. Find out how to look up what you need, and look it up by yourself. Find what you need and quietly go. You need not explain why you desire certain facts.

HAZARDS
ANIMAL, VEGETABLE,
AND   MINERAL

Various animal, vegetable, and mineral hazards may at times confront the THer afield. Forewarned is forearmed, in most cases, and what could be lethally dangerous in ignorance can most often be simply bypassed with rudimentary knowledge. The THing field is exciting enough without sailing blithely into dangers that need not be encountered at all. It is for that reason it is good to consider some of the animal, vegetable, and mineral hazards lurking out there in the boondocks for the unwary THer.

DANGEROUS ANIMALS

The larger animals, unless you get one cornered and have not the sense or opportunity to get out of its way, are not a great danger to people outdoors. Mountain lions, grizzlies and other bears, lynx and bobcats, the antlered great game: All these can be dangerous with jeopardy, but if a person is not careless the chances of his encountering one of these creatures is very, very slim. Tales of dangerous episodes with these wildlife brethren of ours have been blown up out of all proportion to reality in order to embellish novels and magazine stories.

If you ever do meet, face to face, one of our larger beasts, a calm stance, if possible an unhurried retreat, and retention of your wits will probably give the creature time to go on its way. "Tame" bulls are of probably more danger to you than any of the creatures just mentioned, and hogs can even be worse. A gun will probably get you into more problems than it will solve. If you decide to carry one, know how to use it well and quickly, and be willing to face up to irate landowner, forest ranger, game management personnel, or any number of the other meanest, toughest, two-legged critters that roam our land in vast numbers. Use your head and even though you spend most of your life far from the city it is doubtful that you will have much trouble with wild beasts.

Too much has also been said about snakes. Balderdash! We have several different kinds of rattlers in our country; timber rattlers, prairie rattlers, and sidewinders are three of the better known varieties, and water moccasins or cottonmouths, copperheads and coral snakes are the other three poisonous snakes. The Gila monster is the only other poisonous reptile in this country. The danger from all of them can almost entirely be eliminated by wearing good boots and sturdy clothing, watching where one walks, and not acting as though one is in the sterile security of a city park.

If you do happen to manage to be one of the very few snakebite cases the United States has each year, remain calm. Panic circulates the blood with amazing rapidity. If you are bitten, the knowledge that few people die of copperhead or rattlesnake bites **may** make the wound more bearable, but it is doubtful. Avoid it in the first place. Water mocassins are not found out of the southern and southeastern states, and coral snakes live only in parts of the far south, so worry about them only if you live in such areas.

Black widow spiders are a danger to THers, as is the brown recluse spider. This is so because THers have a way of often reaching back into dark corners and crevices. That is the sort of place such spiders spin their webs. The poison works on the nervous system, and is very potent. It can cause a horrible abcess, and if close enough to the heart or brain, death. It is true that a spider cannot inject a great deal of its deadly venom into a person, but it does not take much to make a person extremely sick. One THer east of Wichita, Kansas, a few years back, was exploring an old shed. A black widow bit him, without his even knowing it, right above the right knee. A horrible abcess formed, clear to the bone, and the man was not well for over a year.

The solution is not to stay home, or develop a phobia concerning poisonous spiders. Sturdy clothing takes out most of the risk. Any THer searching old buildings should have gloves with him. Any poking or prying into corners, nooks, and crannies should mean putting them on, without thinking. Such simple measures give amply wide safety margin.

Scorpions are common throughout the southwest, as are centipedes and tarantulas, but although their bites or stings are painful they are not lethal. One exception must be made, and that is the small yellow scorpion. This nasty creature's sting can be fatal, and it is a good thing it is somewhat rare, for at best its stab is extremely painful.

Don't forget about bees, yellow-jackets, and hornets. An encounter with these dive-bombing experts because of a careless moment can be seriously painful and such incidents prove fatal to more people in the

United States each year than all the snakebites combined.

So, all in all, it is the small wildlife you'd best be most aware of, not the great, howling, monstrous beasties.

One should always be careful when looking into cracks and crannies.

BEWARE, THESE PLANTS' BITE IS FAR WORSE THAN THEIR BARK

Some of this world's plant life is downright obnoxious. Some of it, such as some of the simple botulism cells, is lethal, and you can't get much more dangerous than that. We won't go into a long tirade here on watching what you take with you on your expeditions for eats, but we can guarantee that you **should** do so.

In your quest there are a few plant encounters that you may wish to avoid. If you don't avoid them you will wish that you had. The most obvious is poison ivy. In almost all parts of the U.S. and through southern Canada poison ivy grows plentifully, and if you are both often afield and careless you sooner or later will run into it. Literally.

Poison ivy comes in several varieties. Some kinds usually grow rampantly as vines, twining and straggling over ground, tree trunks, and surrounding shrubbery. Other kinds, if they have nothing much on which to climb, form upright bushes. In the Pacific coastal states and in the South, the stuff is more apt to form bushes and clumps than to twine. These are often called poison oak. The leaves of the poision oak are more rounded. Poison ivy leaves come to a sharper point.

Either type can produce the most intensely irritable itching, in case you have never experienced the sensation. It can make a person feel like a pup at a flea circus, or like having on a stiff camel hair shirt inside a Turkish steam bath. Whatever the feeling, it is most definitely not pleasant.

The tissues of these plants extrude a poisonous oil something much like carbolic acid. That's the itching agent, produced by the plant as a protective device. It is not a passive defense! This oil gets onto clothing or skins of people coming into contact with the plants. Careless removal of shoes or clothing after trekking through such vegetation can do the job. Bad cases of poison ivy have been gotten by people walking through smoke from burning poison ivy. Some people are more allergic than others to poison ivy, but it is the better part of valor to avoid the stuff if possible.

Poision ivy is a lovely plant, if one keeps a proper distance. The leaves are bright and shiny green, be they poison oak or ivy. In the Autumn they turn bright red or orange. Each leaf is actually made of three leaflets more or less notched at the edges. One leaf stands by itself at the tip of the leaf, the other two opposite each other on the stalk immediately below it.

Early in the year small greenish flowers grow bunched close to where the leaf begins. In the late summer the flowers are followed by clusters of poisonous berrylike drupes. The drupes are a dingy yellowed white, waxy in the manner of mistletoe berries.

The best thing to do with poison ivy is to avoid it. If, however, you do find yourself one day forcing your way through the nasty stuff, go wash as soon as possible. Handle your clothing and shoes as little as possible. The oil usually takes some time to penetrate the skin, and it does come off with soap and water.

If, after these precaustions fail, and your skin breaks out into an itching, fiery rash, there are things to do besides abandoning all hope and starting to write a will.

The affected areas can be treated with a long-time remedy, and one hard to beat, calamine lotion. This can be gotten at any drugstore. Epsom salts or bicarbonate of soda applications are helpful. A solution of one and one-half teaspoonfuls of potassium permanganate crystals in a pint of water often neutralizes the poison, before and even after the itching starts.

Requiring constant respect throughout the western states, at least, is that large, stickery cactus family. Devil's claw, cholla, prickly pear, and all sorts of other varieties, large and small, bad, vicious, and worse, they all require avoidance. A stumble into a patch of prickly pear will convince anyone that this warning is not idle chatter. Those miserable stickers are all tipped with poison, and the irritation caused by bushing against one of these selfish desert water-hoarders will teach a life-time lesson.

Another vicious plant you by all means should avoid is the 'stinging nettle'. Tom Sawyer's famous encounter with nettles in Mark Twain's tale well illustrates the point. Tom, playing the part of a dying Robin Hood, sank down into some 'stinging nettles', and sprang up far too lively for a corpse.

MINERAL MENACE

Yes, there are some dangerous minerals, and THers should be aware of them. This danger is compounded in caves, which is a risky place to be anyway, unless you are an experienced spelunker exploring with equally experienced companions. In confined spaces dust can be extremely dangerous. Heavy metals can cause all sorts of damage to a person when inhaled. Copper, mercury, or any of a great many metals can be through and through the dust of such places, and easily breathed in by unwary people stirring it up. If your project happens to take you into such places, consider wearing a respirator, or at least a damp bandana around your face. That would be sufficient if you were there for but a short time, and it is doubtful that anyone would see you and have you arrested as a bandito.

Another thing dangerous about certain cave dust, although it is not really mineral, is the terrible fact that rabies can be contracted from bat guano almost as readily as from the bite of a rabid bat.

Perhaps worth mentioning here, although one would think that people would be aware of it, all water is not fit to drink. In heavily mineralized areas some water has high arsenic content, or other mineral pollutants. Not much imagination is required to see what that could do to an unwary, thirsty soul used only to turning on the tap.

TIN CANS & TRASH

(Originally printed in THE TREASURE HUNTERS NEWSLETTER)

Tin cans and trash litter almost any spot the THer wants to explore. Rusted sheet metal rests intertwined with old wire, windrows of rusted tin cans, and tantalizing shards of broken glass. Ancient wash basins, their bottoms eaten away, parts of broken stoves, the bent, scattered pipes that carried the smoke from the stoves, and crcular bits of metal that helped hold tarpaper on the shacks heated by the stoves (circular, almost coin-sized bits of metal).

The picture is familiar to any treasure hunter who has ever approached a potential hunting site. It does not take long to realize that most rusty old tin cans hold more dirt than they do coins. One soon learns that good bottles and other relics also elude discovery. The good things have either been already taken away, broken by nature or vandals, or covered with years of soil and growth accumulations and thereby out of sight underground.

At this point all-too-many THers give up. They put their detectors in their vehicles and go home. The detectors are placed in closets and people give up a great hobby. It is too bad, for these people did not even scratch the surface. Too many folks have the mistaken notion that ghost towns and abandoned sites have been picked clean by somebody else, or have too much junk scattered around to ever find anything valuable. Most often this is not so.

Put on your thinking caps. Realize that anything worthwhile is going to take a certain amount of work as well as thought. If that word "work" does not sound appealing, perhaps you'd best go ahead and store your detector, because THing often does require working up a sweat.

Things get deposited in layers. Examine layers of sedimentary rock sometime, then read about how such materials are formed. Lost and castaway manmade items are little different than trash deposited by natural means. Trash gets deposited in layers, and the items deposited first are in the lowest level, unless disturbed by digging, erosion, earthquake, or some other disruption. Heavy items (such as metal objects) tend to go to the bottom of their respective layers, and succeeding layers tend to hold everything securely in place. All this is to say that a thing is probably right where it was lost or thrown those long year ago. That is where the work comes in, too, with the oldest, more desireable items most often farther down. The top layer, the one the casual observer sees and is disgusted with, the one that makes most would-be treasure hunters give up in disgust and go away, is simply that: THE TOP LAYER.

Tin cans and trash are the beacon that lights the way to adventure for the knowledgeable treasure seekers of the land. Where broken bits of colored glass rest hither and yon there very likely are larger, and perhaps unbroken, glass objects underground. The scattered bits of rusted metal on the surface often indicate the site of a pile of discarded metal objects. Don't snicker. Old tools of yesteryear make excellent collections and displays. Such objects can bring premium prices. They do, that is, if you even desire to sell them, once your own interest in such collectables is stimulated. Old scrap heaps around abandoned farmsteads, sawmills, ranching headquarters, and other such sites often have dozens and dozens of collectables, all of which can be sold, to the right people.

Where are the right people? Flea markets, antique shops, curiosity shops, and individual collectors. Buy a copy of THE ANTIQUE TRADER, a newspaper devoted to the buying and selling of what multitudes of non-knowing folks would call JUNK. The price is 50 cents per copy and their address is P.O. Box 1050, Dubuque, Iowa 52001. A copy may give you some new insights. People pay good money for many of the things one can find, and they will ask if you have more.

So, THers, don't wrinkle your noses at those scattered footing stones, bits of rusty metal, and shards of purpled glass. Ask yourself where the dump was. Where did the house stand, and which way did it face? Coins were often lost around the doorways. Where was the house trash thrown? Most bottles went there. Where was the scrap metal heap. Tools galore are often found in such places, many not really broken. Where was the outhouse?

Ugh! you say? Don't for nasty as it once may have been, it does not take very many years for the contents to reduce to soil. The bottles, coins, and odds and ends that disappeared into that pit are still there. Many folks knew where they lost that coin a hundred years ago, but few desired to go through the then-messy process of recovering it. The process is not messy now. Hard work, perhaps, for the roots of plants grow thick in rich soil, but work that is often well rewarded. It is a good place for several unbroken bottles, especially those that contained strong medicines or poisons. It is also obvious why there often are a few old coins to be found in such places. Think about it for a moment—you will see why.

Many people have taken a look at certain ghost towns where there are no longer any buildings at all, shrugged, and left. Actually there are many advantages to hunting in a place where no buildings remain. I have mentioned in the preceding sentence perhaps the greatest advanmage. Few people even consider hunting there. Also, there is less junk to move from atop where you want to dig.

Speaking of digging, one also must speak of holes. Now if you wish to advertise your activities, and make people angry with you, by all means leave holes. This will make it harder for anyone else to search for what you missed. Landowners have a strange aversion to having dug holes left unfilled on their property. State and federal land management people are not much different. If you get permission to dig on a fellow's property, you should realize the privilege carries with it the responsibility of filling in the holes you dig. It is amazing how much more welcome it makes a person on the man's property. He will have a friendly greeting instead of a shotgun the next time he sees you. He may even remember an even older site, down on the other end of the ranch.

Perhaps this little tirade will help put the tin cans and trash you are bound to encounter a bit more into a proper perspective. In themselves such junky items don't mean much. To the thinking THer, however, they are a guiding light to adventure and recovery.

Some of what's left of Silver City, far up the Alaskan Highway, and a delightful spot.

There are all sorts of caches. This is typical of Alaskan caches, past and present, this one in use at an Indian village downstream from Fairbanks.

34

ECOLOGY AND THE TREASURE HUNTER

Ecology is a big word these days. Most people have greater feelings than knowledge about ecology, but it is a matter of vital importance to all of us. Our old world **is** in trouble. Streets are littered, and as all coinshooters know very well, so are our parks, playing fields, and most other public areas. Fouled streams, dirty air, and cluttered areas are the rule, not the exception.

Ecology is a term meaning how things live together in a given area. Some of our multitude of "new ecologists" haven't the slightest meaning of the term. They rant against the Public Servic Companies and buy more electrical gadgets, a rather contradictory action. They clean the litter from one park and celebrate by having a beer-bust in the other, of course without cleaning up the resulting mess.

THers probably do as much or more than any other sizeable group of people about truly cleaning up their environment. Many coinshooters across the country are personally responsible for picking up several hundred pounds of trash in their jaunts across the nation's playgrounds. They are leaving areas far cleaner than they find them. Bulging coat pockets or brimming full "trash aprons" are no uncommon sights in city parks these days, wherever one may spot one of the species THeritus Americanus. It is done with purely selfish motivation in a few cases, but it does a great public service. The THer knows he will be back, and does not want to pick up the same junk twice. He picks it up and everybody benefits.

This simple act accomplished several things for the THer and his hobby field. It leaves a better image of the hobby. It does leave cleaner recreational areas. Selfishly, whether the THer knows it or not, it makes easier his pursuit of the hobby.

THE DESERT

Desolate vistas of arid land, vast stretches of shifting dunes, miles upon miles of heat-tormentd rocks, distant spires and buttes shimmering in the heat waves—this is what most people envision when they think of deserts. There are these things, and more, in deserts, yet the desert is a good place for those who understand its limits. There are such things as poisonous water holes, bitter salt flats, and wide, dry playa lakes. There are such things as sand storms, scorching days, and chilling nights. These conditions, when properly taken into account, merely are a part of the whole, things that make the desert the singular, and to many people, the beautiful place it is.

Most THers sooner or later will very likely wish to let their hobby lead them into the desert. That is when the pleasures, or the miseries of the dry lands begin. There are many things to look for within the desert lands, far more than lost ledges of gold or silver, abandoned mines, and caches of high grade ore or accumulated money. Isolation is perhaps the greatest gift of the desert in these hectic times, a sense of lonesome privacy now so increasingly hard to come by.

There are things to remember about the desert if one is going to live in it with pleasure instead of misery. First and foremost, the desert is a dry place. A lack of moisture is the determining factor of what is a desert. Not heat, for many deserts are cold. Much of the Arctic is as dry as a dehydrated dribble. There seems to be a lot of moisture because it is too cold for rapid melting and evaporation. Since deserts are dry, it is up to the THer to see to it that he has sufficient water for whatever time he intends to be there. If he doesn't know if there will be water where he is going he should take more than enough along with him, for there probably isn't any water there.

The desert is an awesome place, a rough gem with many facets. A place such as this can be blazing hot, but Ken Marquiss says at the time this photo was taken it was bitterly cold. (A Gold Hex photo)

MOUNTAINS

It has been said of many mountains, "How breathtaking!" Many a THer knows how true that statement is. If one does much hiking around those mountains, they are, indeed, breathtaking. Everything seems up, including one's pulse.

Most THers, sooner or later, encounter mountains in the pursuit of their interest. The reason is simple enough. Mining activities were concentrated in the heavily mineralized zones of the more mountainous areas. Cliffs, faults, and the greater erosional rates normal to steep slopes expose a greater variety of ores than usually can be found in flatter areas.

There are problems attached to working in the mountainous areas other than shortness of breath. Anyone dealing with the mountains, be they tenderfoot or long term native, should be well aware of such a region's special problems. Rapidly changeable weather conditions, varying steepness of slope, loose and falling rocks, avalanche, the swiftness and coldness of streams, and dozens of other factors should be fully realized by those who head for the hills.

One of the first things one notices while climbing a mountain is that the higher one goes the colder it becomes. It doesn't seem right. The first thought is, should not the temperature rise as one gets closer and closer to the sun? Not so, the air is thinner and usually drier with increased altitude. It absorbs much less heat than air farther downslope. Temperature is lowered an average of three degrees Fahrenheit for every 1,000 feet of elevation above sea level. This makes available extra clothing necessary.

Such clothing cannot just be put on and forgotten, though. One finds it must be put on, taken off, put on, taken off, with absolutely no predictibility. Sun can blister the skin at high altitudes, too, even though little heat is felt. Ultraviolet rays come blistering down onto exposed skin areas little filtered out by the thinner atmosphere. The THer expecting to do work at higher elevations would be well forewarned to do, as many skiers do, go into the mountains with a jar of cold cream.

Temperature variation is great, and so is the variation in precipitation. Amount, variability, dependability, and type is simply unpredictable. It can be sunny, rain, blow, snow, sleet, cloud over, become fogged in, and all this between sunrise and sunset, high in the mountains. Conditions can last, and they can change within moments. Therefore waterproof as well as warm clothing is most advisable, as are plenty of changes. Wet clothing in cold weather is not only miserable, it is dangerous to health.

Undoubtedly the most constantly dangerous enemy of man on a mountain is slope. Slope is a passive foe, but constantly working on the intruder upon the mountain. Gravity makes everything harder. That relentless force constantly pulls downslope. It makes tiresome the climb and wearisome the descent. The least forgetfulness can turn a braked crawl into a shattering fall. That everlasting drag can crash man down upon things, or things down upon man, and one should never forget that fact.

The skier uses the slope, of course, and this is mentioned because it brings up a THing possibility few people have seemed to consider. Winter time is not really all that bad a time to go treasure hunting. Snowshoes and snow vehicles also fall under this heading.

Some excellent THing sites are snowed in a good share of the year. Access is virtually impossible during the winter months except to equipment designed to cope with such conditions. Given access, these sites have an isolation beyond belief if one sees those same spots during the summer months. Such isolation means leisurely if somewhat limited searching. It is worth mentioning, and many THers might consider carefully adopting such a technique in certain instances.

Another hazard, already indirectly mentioned, is the reduced ability of easy breathing at higher altitudes. Most people are used to almost fifteen pounds of air pressure to the square inch at or around sea level. If that is considered 100% of desirable air pressure it should be realized that at five thousand feet above sea level there is only 83% that much air pressure. Denver, Colorado, is 300 feet higher than that. At 10,000 feet above sea level, and that is where a good many old mining areas are, there is only 67% of the sea level air pressure. That, THers, is why you have such a hard time catching your breath. You may be getting 15% less oxygen than you're used to receiving. Shortness of breath, headaches, fatigue and sometimes nosebleeds are common results. More dramatic symptoms may indicate that THing at that altitude is not really the thing to do.

Fortunately, most THers do not fall into that category, and somewhat like easing into hot water, they can work up to it. It is rushing into the mountains that makes for misery, just as jumping into hot water would make for misery.

Built about 1905, one of the first cabins in the Circle, Alaska area. One of the builders, hungry in the spring for something green, picked a mess of what he thought was wild celery. It wasn't, and he died to prove it.

SWAMPS

Unlike the desert, swamplands have water; more than enough water. Boat replaces four-wheeled drive, waders replace sturdy hiking boots, mosquito repellant replaces suntan oil, and everything gets lugged around in waterproof containers. These soggy places have their share of leads, for such areas have many hide-out type locations, often used for just such purposes, and many a recluse has lived out a hermit-like life in some shack set on a high-dry spot.

Bottle hunters for years have found swampy areas profitable depositories. What better place to throw an empty bottle? How often does a bottle break when it hits the muck?

It's often the high-dry spots, though, where the small caches are apt to be. True, there have been some castiron pots located, held in their place for years by a wire, a chain, or sometimes—for a while—by a rope. Nevertheless, most caches are where the depositor could get at them easily when he wished or needed to do so, not out in the oozy goo. Any rise of land that was once inhabited bears close scrutiny.

The swamplands are well worth looking at, THers, even though it is hardly the same operation as mountain or desert projects.

OLD MINES

Old mines are interesting places. Some may still contain potential additions to the THer's bank account, often not directly connected with the material originally mined there. There are other metals than gold, silver, copper, lead, and so forth, and rare earths of exceedingly high value: Things old time miners never even dreamed of. They took out their gold, and often walked out those shafts for the last time over incredible values.

No matter how fascinating such crumbled old shafts and drifts may be, however, they are also exceedingly dangerous. Unwary THers are subject to all sorts of perils.

One of my close friends told me a tale the other day that made my hackles rise, and I think my reaction startled her. I hope so! She is very attractive and her husband, I am sure, would miss her a great deal.

The young lady has gotten very interested this past year in the entire THing world, and especially in old ghost towns and areas around abandoned mines. It seems she had found an odd little stone building, one weekend, a sturdy but completely rusted padlock still holding fast a still strong door. She poked and pried around, and even ran a metal probe in through cracks in the door.

"I would really like to know what that little house was for," said she.

I told her that she had described a rather common sort of powder house, a place where the miners stored their explosives. As hopeless a punster as I am, when I saw that expression on her face, I refrained saying, "You might have gotten a real bang out of that." Old dynamite is wicked stuff, as any old miner will tell you, let alone corroded blasting caps. Old black powder, when it is dry, retains huge explosive power.

Another incident that happened just south of Central City, Colorado, points out another literal pitfall connected with old mines. Three young men took their Jeep on the mined-over hill south of Nevadaville one snowy day three winters ago. They parked their vehicle to explore the old mine buildings. One boy got out the side opposite the driver and disappeared into a two hundred or so foot shaft, straight down. The recent storm had completely hidden the open shaft with a snow bridge. Six feet to the right and the Jeep would have gone in. They recovered the young explorer's body.

Old mines often have vertical shafts. Don't count on seeing and avoiding them, either. Many such shaft was covered with a sturdy wooden cover. The alternating damp and dry conditions that are often found in mines cause an inevitable deterioration of wood. Old timbers, ancient props, and crumbling shaft covers sometimes fall into dust and slivers at a touch. Falling props often preced collapsing walls and timbers.

Never go into mines alone, if you must go, and you should preferably get the help and advice of a mining engineer. You might be lucky enough to find an old-timer who worked in the mine, or at least knew it. His knowledge might help you anticipate what of value might still be found there, too.

The foundations of one of the saloons at Sunshine, Colorado, once a rich producer of gold. A three dollar gold piece was lost down the cracks in the flooring several years before the establishment burnt down, and very likely is still there. Perhaps with other coins of the 1880's.

An apology is perhaps in order concerning the large number of pictures dealing with the Colorado scene. The author just happens to live in Boulder, Colorado. By rights there should be scenes from every state, every section of the country, but if the readers will do a bit of mental substitution, they can surely see parallels within their own counties, their own towns. One of the great joys of THing is that in all its differences and variations a THer, as he gains experience, begins to see the recurring similarities.

CAVES

Caves have long been the shelter of man, home long prior to shingled roofs and brick hearths. THers will undoubtedly at one time or another be tempted to enter such a place, large or small, for caves have often proven to be excellent treasure sites. Artifacts, caches of money or other valuables, weapons, and all sorts of intriguing items were often left in caves, accidentally or on purpose. The depositors sometimes did not return. Remarkable recoveries have been made these past few years from the dark and hidden nooks and crannies of certain caves.

It does not pay to rush carefree and heedless into caves, however. Such places can prove to be death traps. The unwary, especially, can be crushed by falling rocks, gassed by lethal fumes, drowned in sudden floods, bitten by snakes, fall into unseen depths, and many, many other unpleasant things. If go into a cave you think you must, and perhaps there is a good reason for it, by all means take a knowledgeable partner or two, a person who knows the dangers and how best to cope with them. Do your research before you search, and make certain you really need to enter the cave-world.

Caves can be very interesting, of course, and THers do have a way of coming across reasons to enter such places. Of the two, natural caves are more often safe than old mines, but both places require one's utmost caution and respect.

THE OUTHOUSE

Shudder not, THer, when the subject of digging into the past via the old outhouse pit is mentioned. The contents of such an establishment return to soil in only a few years, and the outhouses that may contain items people consider to be collectables have been abandoned for longer than only a few years; most often decades have passed since those thrones of relief were used.

Why dig in such a repulsive spot is a question I often have heard, a lip at times slightly upturned in disgust, a doubtful cast of the eye indicating revulsion, and general bewilderment obvious to the most casual observer, let alone to anyone who has seen this typical reaction many times. It is a logical question for someone to ask, especially if they have not previously thought about the subject. Outhouses do, somehow, seem to reek of things other than treasure.

First let me repeat a statement all THers have heard phrased and paraphrased many times: Where people congregate, spend a good deal of time, and have their minds somewhere else, that's a good place to find things. Outhouses qualify. Surely you've seen the old two or even three holers. I have even seen fancied-up seats with holes cut for Dad, Mom, and junior. Perhaps misery loves company.

If you want to find old bottles the outhouse pit definitely ought to be considered as a prime target. Strong medicine, and old or doubtful medicines went into the pit, for that was one place the kiddies would not accidently retrieve the noxious stuff and possibly poison themselves. Poison bottles went into the pit. Any container with potential dangers could safely be deposited therein without fear of the little ones getting hold of it.

One of my friends, who lives in a small town east of Boulder, took my advice and dug into some old outhouse pits in several of the old coal camps. He found bottles, and they were good ones. Not being a bottle collector, Gene sold them. One he got $18.00 for at the antique auction they have in that small town each week. When he described the bottle we looked it up in a book and found the lady who'd purchased it now has a $30.00 bottle, but Gene felt amply rewarded.

Bottles are not the only thing to be found in the old pits. Coins have been and are found in those locations. Pennies and nickels usually suffer under the somewhat adverse conditions they endure, but silver and gold coins as a rule suffer little or no change at all over the years.

The same fellow also made in one of the coal camp outhouse pits a rather remarkable recovery. From one shovelful of dry, crumbly, rich earth tumbled an engraved, collapsable silver drinking cup. It had the lid,

and in itself was a great find. Gene shook it, and it rattled. Opening it, his hands trembling with understandable excitement, a dozen coins rolled into his upturned palm. A 1902 Canadian dime, several V nickels, two or three Indian head pennies, a walking liberty quarter, and several barber dimes. That small trove paled into insignificance, however, as he saw the other three items he held. There was a gold wedding band, an engagement ring with three good diamonds, the center one perhaps half a carat, and a fine diamond solitaire broach. It was old filagree gold, the kind popular around the turn of the century, which is reasonable considering the fact that the coal camps were going strong at that time.

What was something like that doing in an outhouse pit? Who knows? That is exactly what makes treasure hunting such an exciting activity and why such sites as abandoned outhouse pits are worth careful excavation. Perhaps the man's wife ran off with another man. Maybe the children dropped it down there accidentally and were afraid to admit or tell about it. For sure, it would make quite a story, if one could know how such a thing happened. A THer often has to be a fairly good detective, archaeologist, and analyst rolled into one, and have a rather good imagination to boot.

Another man, a professional seeker of treasure, who cannot be named in conjunction with this tale, found a cache in an old outhouse. Yes, a cache, and a very good one. It makes sense, and it was very well done. It is well worth mentioning.

The THer heard the story about an uncle who was supposed to have had a lot of money, but no money turned up after his death. The family, which consisted of nephews and neices only, for the old man had lived out his life as a bachelor, tore the place apart after his funeral, but never found a cent. Years passed, and the THer heard the stoy, got the location, and decided it was a good lead.

For two days he was no more successful than had been the heirs. Then he took a closer look at the outhouse, and there it was. The old man had carefully constructed a good wooden partition off to one side of the pit, not directly beneath the hole. A wide-mouth metal jug, a chain through its handle and held by a large nail to a beam beneath the seat, held several thousand dollars in gold and silver coins. The old gentleman only had to go out to the outhouse, reach through the hole and to one side, and pull up his jug. After subtracting or adding to the hoard he could swing it back into its neat little hidey-hole, out of the way, and certainly out of the sight of people. Not many folks make a habit of poking their heads down into outhouse holes when that establishment is in active use.

How long this was the old man's depository of wealth is not known, but from the contents of the jug it must have gone on for years.

Not all outhouses have that sort of treasure, of course, but the story should illustrate something worthwhile to the thinking THer. These sites have the possibility of containing many little treasures, and at times could yield items of truly great value.

LAW AND THE TREASURE HUNTER

Make no mistake about it, laws are to be obeyed. People who break laws often themselves get broken. We can choose to break laws, for we are creatures of free choice, but there are penalties for the breaking of laws. If one chooses to step or leap off a high place, deciding the law of gravity is not relevant for him, the penalty is severe. Often it is instantaneous capital punishmen. One may choose to break the caloric laws, and the penalties are often obesity, high blood-pressure, hardening of the arteries, and/or any number of other unpleasant results.

These are natural laws, of course, and we are talking about man made laws and the treasure hunter, but the analogy holds true. For there are, also, plenty of natural laws the THer darned well best keep in mind, and the text of this book deals with a few of them. There are laws dealing to varying extents with treasure hunting in different states, and it is to a THer's best interests to be aware of both the laws and their effects.

There are some laws, and what is even worse, bureaucratic decrees and edicts that compound, surpass, confuse, and replace laws affecting treasure hunting. Such conditions and such laws can be changed, but the THer should be careful in careful in willfully breaking such laws before they are changed. Where unjust laws and petty, harrassing bureaucratic rule and regulation need change, THers should band together and fight to acheive such change. Banging one's head up against bureaucracy is about the same as banging the noggin on a brick wall, and gets similar results. Lumps, black and blue marks, and headaches. Therefore, know the law, stay within it, and work by yourself and with other THers to get poor laws abolished or changed for the better.

HERE'S WHAT TO TELL ABOUT YOUR THing ACTIVITIES

Button your lip, close your mouth, develop acute laryngitis, pause between hems and haws, and overall, keep what you know to yourself. A big, flapping mouth has ruined many an excellent recovery. All too often someone who has made the mistake of bragging about what he is in the process of recovering goes to the spot and finds evidence that somebody was all ears. No treasure, no thank-you note, no nothing save perhaps a hole, a misplaced board or brick, some freshly turned earth, or a set of tire tracks, coming and going.

An urge to boast of success, impending or achieved, is going to lead to trouble. Someone may be looking for the same thing, and with what you say, quickly and quietly beat you to the punch. All sorts of persons, should you make a find public, will want to share your new-found wealth. Some will haul you into court, claiming it as solely or partially theirs.

This THing, especially near the time of recovery, is truly a case of: SILENCE IS GOLDEN, WHY NOT GET RICH? Just shut up and go about your business. Everyone does not need to know all you're doing. It is **your** business, and it's best to keep it that way.

Pay attention to such signs. If you really want to hunt such a place, seek permission. That is often all one has to do.

TRESPASS

There will be times that it is inconvenient to get permission to hunt on a particular piece of property. You know the owner is out of town. You've heard he's a crusty old buzzard. He's a Republican and you're a Democrat, or vice-versa. You'd have to drive twenty miles over to the main ranch house. On and on could go the reasons.

The signs say NO TRESPASSING, Violators will be prosecuted, PRIVATE PROPERTY, and **KEEP OUT.** Too many people ignore the signs and trespass anyway. They get away with it, sometimes. Sometimes they don't, too, and even if they do there's always that uncomfortable crawling sensation up and down your spine. The least noise, a cloud of dust over the nearby hill, sounds of traffic coming down an isolated road; anything of that sort and the heart begins to pound and the mouth gets dry.

Don't trespass. It is not all that complicated or difficult to get permission to hunt most private property. Straight, honest approaches are the best. Absolute respect of other peoples' property while you're hunting completes the circle, and new friends have been made. We have the ownership of private property in this country, and praises be for that fact. Think about it for awhile, and you will see tremendous advantages in that situation for THers. There are a great many pieces of private property around this vast land of ours that have never yet heard the beep of a metal detector nor felt the trod of a treasure seeker's feet.

You may have the give the real reason for wanting to hunt on his property to the landowner and you may not. Don't spill all the beans if you don't have to. Many people will consider you sort of a nut, but they will actually enjoy seeing you "hunt for farm tools and other artifacts." They won't mind if you coinshoot around where Uncle Joe had his house before it burned down. If you have reason to believe Uncle Joe may have buried a cache before the present owners were even born you should not feel compelled to blab all you know.

Sometimes the most practical, best way of searching for a particular cache is to sign a search and salvage agreement. That way everything is spelled out clearly. An understanding is reached prior to the search. If you feel there may be the slightest hint of suspecting your real motive I would not hesitate to enter such an agreement. A shade of distrust and doubt soon breeds intense greed and dislike. You could be ordered off the place, and physical violence is possible.

In such a case trespass can become extremely dangerous, and a person is foolish to rush in where angels in bullet-proof vests would fear to tread. Trespassers who've had previous words with landowners have been known to be verbally assaulted, severely beaten, or even shot.

None of this is necessary. If you do reach a dead end, and not even a search/salvage agreement is of help, shelve the project. If you really want to get on that land try to think of safe, legal methods. Rent the place, if you can. Offer to buy some used building materials, chop and saw some cordwood, haul out some topsoil or gravel, or any plausible reason. Make it something useful, and you will probably end up with enough opportunity to do your looking. If none of these work, table the project for however long it takes. I am something of a fatalist, I suppose, for I have the feeling that things that are supposed to be usually work out.

If you feel as though you are rowing up a waterfall with only a ping pong paddle, perhaps it is time to begin another project.

GHOST TOWNING

There's all sorts of exploring and adventure in ghost towns, but there's really not too many ghosts. One is more apt to find cows in ghost towns than ghosts. Eerie noises usually turn out to be packrats or chipmunks. Something flitting from one sagging building to another is more likely a blue jay than a wraith. Rattling noises turn ut to be stones clattering down the nearby hillside from a passing band of sheep, not chains in the dank cellars. Few apparitions appear in these deserted abodes of men.

Nevertheless, with the slightest bit of imagination, one can almost see the shades of people past walking up and down those now ill-defined streets. The wind, at times, can almost seem to be the wistful whispers of long ago residents, bemoaning the decay and neglect of a once booming place. Weathered boards, gilded anew by golden sunset or crimson dawn briefly regain the bright zest of a frontier town building up to a future that somehow disappears, and the "guest" of the abandoned townsite sighs with the ghosts of those long gone to so witness the fading of a great and gaudy scene.

It is not difficult to realize why these deserted sites are called ghost towns. Abandoned, often almost reclaimed by the environment within which heedless settlers raised it, these ruins are mere "ghosts" of what they were for a few short years. Hardly a memory remains of the sturdy, adventurous souls who walked the streets, and where traffic bustled, now weeds grow rank.

It is surprisingly difficult, though, to say just what a ghost town is, for it is not just one thing. A few old towns did not die, remained increasingly busy, and today are going as strong as ever, if not more so. Revived by new mining interests, renewed by tourist trade, located strategically, such places somehow don't seem much like what most of us think ghost towns should be.

This flat foundation area may not look promising. It is all that is left of a rooming house at the stone-quarrying town on Noland, Colorado. The site has produced many artifacts, an interesting trade token, some Indian head cents, and a gold locket. Other such sites can be equally rewarding to careful coinshooting.

Central City, Colorado, Virginia City, Nevada, and many other of the old gold camps kept busily alive by tourists all throughout the west are definitely not ghosts. Born of the same era, with enough nostalgic aura remaining, though repainted and repaired, these towns are far more alive than dead. Aspen, Crested Butte, and Breckenridge are all towns that perhaps would have become more ghostly had not skiing made them boom in ways that mining never did.

The reasons for visiting ghost towns are many. Most THers like to seek out deserted townsites, but for nearly as many different reasons as amongst the general population. Some go simply to look, out of curiosity, and that really is reason enough. Some go to vandalize. For those wretches, shame, and would it not be true justice for real ghosts to rise up, chains clanking and mouldy bones rattling, and drive those desecrators shrieking homewards. Some go to take photographs, others to draw or paint. Others seek bottles or other artifacts. A few come to coinshoot. The reasons are many, but they have the spirit of adventure in common.

These ghost towns, the ones isolated and still standing, are suffering a senility that will not linger long. Many of us find this a sad fact, for the seeking out of ghost towns is a fine sport and a zestful avocation.

Merely visiting the old sites is no mean use of time. There are many people who "collect" ghost towns by reading of them, driving there, hiking and poking about, and then going on to another, hopefully even less known and more difficult to find. Such a hobby is no stranger than mountain climbing, or spelunking, or birdwatching.

Vandalism is an even worse enemy of ghost towns than Mother Nature, which is saying a great deal, and it is absolutely uncalled for. These old towns are falling apart rapidly enough with only the savage blows of nature. Snows, blows, forest fires, gravity, decay, and a hundred other large and small circumstances grind apart these places a bit more each year. Pea-brained vandals accelerate the process, and don't think for a moment that such thoughtless, wretched acts don't work to the detriment of THers. There is a great deal of nostalgic, and well-deserved, feeling for these relics of yesteryear, and such fiery feeling, fanned by senseless, destructive vandalism, could easily pour water on THers' ghost towning fever.

Several ghost towns have disappeared before the clandestine onslaught of pry bars and hammers wielded by Colorado's new "mountain people" and "old lumber sellers" alike. Such individuals seek free lumber, one group to rebuild old cabins and shacks and acquire the firewood with which to heat them, the other group to make a few extra dollars. Neither goal is unworthy, but it is if at the expense of our ghost towns and those folks who enjoy visiting the sites. Upon public lands these places may be situated, but that gives nobody the free rein to go in and dismantle them board and joist. Such activities are abruptly erasing from the face of the

Rockies, and I am sure elsewhere, many picturesque sites. Shacks bent and broken by winter snows are there one week, gone the next, every plank and stick.

Another destructive force eliminating many old cabins should be mentioned, for not much publicity has been given it, and people should know. The forest service has been tearing down and burning a great many old cabins all through the western states. They do not want them being lived in. "Hippies" moved into some of the old shacks at Tiger, not far from Breckenridge. They began to repair them enough to withstand the elements. The forest service promptly told them to move. The bulldozer was to go in as the hippies left. At this writing that particular issue has not been solved, but I personally cannot see much difference in the cabins being torn down by the "hippies" or the cabins being torn down by the forest service. The cabins are gone, whichever way.

The forest service claims this action returns the land to its more normal state. Perhaps that is true. If that line of reasoning is followed very far, however, a severe plague would eliminate enough people to make it feasible for large-scale slum clearance and resulting extensive greenbelt development. A government-induced famine could clear out entire areas and return them to its more normal state. Such reasoning, **I hope,** may be far fetched, but many of us think we should not act like sheep. Sheep get sheared.

Nothing lasts forever, and that is most true of the old ghost towns, but there seems little or no sense in speeding the process. One can find few of the remarkable ghost towns drawn by Muriel Wolle in her STAMPEDE TO TIMBERLINE or MONTANA PAY DIRT in the 1940's. Most of such buildings are gone.

The camera offers a remarkably effective method of "collecting" ghost towns. The resulting pictures will undoubtedly outlast their subject, and such as the African camera safari, one does not have to destroy the subject to enjoy it. It actually allows those who cannot get out to such places to share some of the adventure of being there. Robert Brown is another author who has done an excellent job with his Coloado ghost town books. His photography of such sites is very good, and has helped many a peson to locate various spots they otherwise might never have found.

One does not have to be a professional photographer to enjoy using a camera to collect the essence of these places. Just remember to take your camera along when you go. Even the less expensive cameras, when directed by interest and enthusiasm, will produce fine shots, but not if the equipment is left at home.

Artwork offers another means of ghost towning. Be it paint, chalk, water colors, pencil, or something else, a picture can capture nuances of a place no camera can match. Muriel Wolle is a good example of such sketches put to good use, but legion are those who've transferred ghost towns to paper and a wall to hang observed and appreciated long after the real thing falls into weed-choked decay. All of us are not artists, but for those who to any degree are, ghost towns furnish many an excellent subject.

If coinshooting is a primary concern in your seeking out ghost towns, be prepared to work at it. As a rule, if you want sheer numbers of coins, stay in your local park. Those old time streets are not paved with gold and silver, and copper is hard enough to come by. You will find more trash than artifacts, more artifacts than coins. Even so, there is some fine numismatic material still to be found in those sites of years ago. One coin lost right out of circulation onto the dusty streets of a town doomed to oblivion makes coinshooting ghost towns far more interesting than searching any park for new coins. How can one describe the feeling of getting the several hundredth signal, probing, and bringing up a pre-1900 coin. There is a gem, looking as good as new! One cannot help but quickly look around for the fellow who dropped it. Then, with a shake of the head, you put your prize in your pocket and go back to work, for that person is probably no longer living. When you do this the first time, you will see why these places are called **ghost** towns.

Bottles, artifacts, coins, photographs, paintings, or whatever, ghost towning is a most pleasurable avocation. Frustrating at times. Sad, oftentimes. Exciting, nostalgic, and a continuing challenge, ghost towning is one of the many adventures of treasure hunting.

One of the cabins at Champagne, one of the old Canadian fur-trading posts. The site is bisected by the Alaskan highway, and the original terrain has been dulldozed every which way, yet some of the old structures away from the roadbed are still much as they have been for years.

There are good finds to be made in ghost towns by persistent coinshooters. These eight coins, and miscellaneous trinkets, were among nineteen found at Camp Francis, Colorado in an area probably less than fifty square feet. It was where either the old bar or the general store had stood, though nothing more than a basement pit and a leveled foundation area was left to show that it had once been a busy spot

ADVERSE STATE AND FEDERAL ACTIONS AGAINST THing

If life is a bed of roses, which is somewhat doubtful, there's quite a few thorns amongst those lovely petals! One of the worst problems facing any THer today is the mish-mash mess of federal, state, and local actions involving treasure hunting. When a THer or group of THers recover something is when the fur usually flies. Many who've had this experience feel as though they have been trying to turn somersaults in vinegar-flavored January molasses. As long as a THer doesn't find anything much, all seems well, but lands-to-goodness if he should find anything of value and make the mistake of saying anything to anybody about it.

A complete account of the bureaucratic mess we're in these days cannot be given here, but a few items will be sufficient to show the drift of the wind. The rank aroma of needless governmental agency harassment, unlegislated departmental decree and edict, and blindly burgeoning misuse of officialdom is wrinkling far more noses than just those of treasure hunters across this land. Laws are one thing, self-seeking, bureaucratic, dictatorship by those who supposedly are hired by those they attempt to rule by regulation is another.

Read a copy of Rocky LeGaye's Jaye Smith Defense Committee booklet, THE NEW PADRE ISLAND STORY. I am proud to be a member of that committee. We intend to see that fight right up through the Supreme Court, if need be, to win our first class citizens' rights. Riff-raff several thousand strong can raise hell, send up marijuana smoke signals advertising their orgies, and the rangers look the other way on Padre Island. It has happened many times. Let one young lady with a metal detector, however, looking for a sun-blackened Spanish piece of eight, tread upon those sands, look out. Jaye Smith, ticketed upon the spot, must be guilty of desecrating the national heritage and vandalizing the national seashores with a table knife. Her detector was confiscated, as many others across the country have been, not for breaking a law, but for violating a bureaucratic decree.

A few local parks and state parks have been closed to THers. Granted, it was getting pretty bad in a few places. Most of us are pretty careful of picking up trash and leaving a place better than we found it, but there have been and are a few jerks in our hobby field who care not for any save themselves—and they probably are the ones who yowl the loudest when the no THing signs go up.

Sacajawea Park, east of Pasco, Washington, for instance was closed to THing a few years ago. The local THers grimaced, took it in stride, and found other sites. What did not set well at all, when found out at a later date, is that park personnel **who had their own detectors** have been enjoying their private hunting grounds before and after work hours. This is absolute misuse of position, and is far too common in this supposed land of equal rights. Safe in civil servant positions, too many bureaucrats have increasingly been cornering privilege and position with neat, simple little rules and decrees.

The incident where some California men hauled a huge boulder of jade out of a beach cave still rankles most of us when we think about it. The state of California took the attitude that any profits from that glorious stone belonged entirely to the state of California.

Texas lawmakers have made it virtually impossible to work **with** the state in artifact recovery. In doing so they simply encourage clandestine action or hunting on private land: Private landholders are more reasonable people than the "leaders" of Texas lately have seemed to be.

One point must be made. Most of our elected officials really try to do a good job for the people they represent. They will listen to you if you call or write, and YOU SHOULD, AS OFTEN AS POSSIBLE when adverse actions are pending. It is the servants we must fear, for bureaucracy is closer to being our actual rulers in this country than most folks realize. Many of our senators and representatives know this, and need our backing to straighten things out. Be willing to give them that help or be willing to see increasing bureaucratic controls.

The impact of these controls upon THing is different from place to place. Some federal lands, for instance, are still fairly open to such activities. Others, such as the Superstition Mountains, may well be closed soon to any but the most secretive and sneaking of treasure hunts, and most of those I know in this field really aren't that kind of folks. Some of the Great Lakes are closing down on scuba diving and beach combing. There are places I don't see how even the bravest THer/scuba diver could stand to dive, anyway, the waters have become so fouled, but the same bureaucratic impulse to stifle private endeavor runs strong.

What can you do. Don't be passive. Speak out, write, express your views. That or accept regimentation. Let your elected officials know that THers are a strong hobby field, want to do things properly, want to preserve, not destroy our American heritage, and are as much or more interested in archeology than archeologists. Just don't wait for others to do it, for it is going to take a strong, concerted effort amongst us all to maintain the THing hobby field in this country against the bureaucratic machinery that seems bent upon trampling it down.

The rancher was going to burn this old house to the ground. Note the hand-squared logs. They are bringing up to $4 to $5 *per linear foot.* The weathered one inch boards are in demand, too. Money in the pocket is better than ashes on the ground, even if it is sad when these old places are torn down.

ANTIQUES AND AMERICANA

When you go treasure hunting you will find more "stuff" than you do coins. Hasten not to the trash bin, at least not until you look carefully at what you've found. Roy Lagal states that he has been a treasure hunter all his life, but that most of his income of the bread and butter variety has come from selling "junk". "Junk hunting for a living" is the way he puts it.

Most full time seekers of treasure soon discover the same thing. They simply cannot depend on recovering enough caches to make a steady, dependable living. Supplemented by sales of "trash" it has proven feasible for many to do what they like and not starve to death. Don't try it unless you're really willing to work, though, and are willing to keep up on the values of things found. Treasure hunters just cannot get away from constant researching, not even if they are dealing with artifacts and antiques. There is simply no sense in selling something for $5.00 that should and could have been sold for $25.

THing is an activity with many facets. Many searchers have specialized in bottles, and done very well at it. Legion are those who've never really given a thought to coins and caches, but have had excellent yearly incomes from going across country acquiring antiques and reselling them. One man, beginning in Dallas and creating a marvelous business salvaging materials from buildings being demolished, moved to Georgia, started a second, larger business there. He spends part of each year touring Europe seeking old buildings to be torn down. The things he brings back in the way of materials are simply amazing, and much of it would have been junked if he had not purchased it.

A good share of the so-called "trash" that many novice THers pick up and promptly throw back down is marketable. It has a cash value to somebody. The problem for the treasure hunter is to know what he has, something of its value, and where he might most profitably sell it.

I have picked up ox shoes that others before me have dug up and thrown away thinking they were broken horseshoes. I have sold several of these for a five dollar bill apiece, and talking with a fellow here in Boulder who has a collection of ox and horse shoes, I find that some of them could be worth much more.

One friend, in Denver, located a short spur of a railroad on the Western Slope here in Colorado where they used a novel railroad spike. It was wide one way, very narrow the other, and had a nail-like head above the top flange. He sold fifty of them to an antique store on Larimer Square in Denver for $2.00 each. He was using a Garrett Mini-Hunter, and had debated before buying it whether or not he would ever get his purchase price back in what he found. He doubts no longer.

The author does not know a great deal about antiques, but he does know that when one finds something unusual he ought to find out what it is before destroying or discarding it. A THer in Lafayette, Colorado, just this past fall found an embossed bottle. He got $18 for it at the local auction. Less than two weeks later he discovered that the bottle was valued at approximately $35. A realtor acquaintance of mine bought an old house as an investment. There was a good deal of old furniture the former owner, an older lady, left because she was entering a nursing home. The realtor broke up one marred, beat-up bedroom set and had it all hauled away to the dump. Later a neighbor woman stopped by to ask the realtor if he would take a couple hundred dollars for that birdseye maple bedroom set the old lady had left.

Bitter salt tears don't wash back the lost dollars carelessness swept away.

If you are to make any money from "junk" you have to know to some degree what you are finding. Knowledge is the only way this lost or tossed-away stuff can be labeled, a market for it found, and a reasonable price tag decided. A thing is worth what one can get for it, but contrary to popular belief the world does not beat a path to the door of the inventor of a better mousetrap—not unless he gets the word out TO THE RIGHT PLACES that he has perfected such an invention. The THer has to be able to go to the right "market" to get the best price for his various finds.

For some recoveries there is no better place than odds and ends shops, junktique stores, etc. Clock shops, key shops, hardware stores: Specialized stores are a good place to sell specialized items. Many a drugstore operator would be willing to part with many $$$ for a few good, really old implements, bottles, jars and so forth of his trade, for use as display. Restaurants, bars, museums, and other such businesses dealing in display and human interest are natural outlets for a THer's "trash". The **atmosphere** of many places has to be created by something other than cigarette smoke and alcohol fumes. Old tools, weapons of years ago, bits and pieces of Americana are just the things to help a place create such an atmosphere. Your job is to become the best possible salesman of your to such places. If you can truly say, "This came from a stage stop, this came from the old minging town of _____, and this was dug up near the foundations of Gerties Haven for Misguided Maidens." you probably can make a sale for a sum most people who saw you dig up those things would never believe.

Now Knowledge does not come easy. You have to do some reading, or ask some old timers. Old folks often can glance at a whatzit, and say, "Sure, that's an adjustable bung borer—I ain't seen one of those dern things since I worked at Uncle Zeke's orchard," or, "My golly, if that isn't a hogshead champer. Where did you get that?"

62

There are a good many helpful identification books. One such good book, although there are others, is Old Time Bottles Publication's 1865 Wishbook. If you are really serious about making some money you ought to have such a book in your personal library, or know that it's available in your library.

Speaking of libraries, here's a suggestion. You've all heard that the squeaky wheel gets the grease. Well, now, make a few suggestions of books you would like your library to have. Most librarians truly want to serve their clients. They are very receptive to suggestions to book acquisitions. If you really would like them to purchase a particular title, you tell them. Then ask half a dozen or more of your friends to do the same thing. Not on one day, but over a two or three week period. If the book is in print you will probably see it on the library's shelves fairly quickly. Don't expect overnight miracles, of course.

Should you get interested in specialized antiques, be it china, furniture, glassware, or whatnot, the books on such subjects are simply astonishing in number. Send off for a sample copy of THE ANTIQUE TRADER, Dubuque, Iowa 52001. It's 50¢ for a single copy, and has so much information of various antique and other books and dealers that one has to read a copy to believe it. By browsing through a single issue you can probably locate a book or two to answer all sorts of specialized questions.

This is worth mentioning, because any THer afield is apt to come across a veritable horde of some particular item. What does one do with a half pickup load of sawmill tools? What value does a shoebox full of door hardware have? What price should sixteen unchipped dishes with a most unusual pattern, obviously very old, bring? This sort of problem could be any THer's. What's fun is to make it a happy profit. It is not fun to later find out you gave away a bonanza.

A few words here about caution in recovery, cleaning, and repair are probably in order. Other books go into detail on these subjects, but this warning, if heeded, could add many dollars to your pocket.

Fist of all, in spite of digging up lots of things that are simply trash and becoming bored, be careful in your recovery methods. A carelessly weilded shovel has often marred beyond value an otherwise worthwhile artifact. If you are in a good spot there is no such thing as being too careful. Shovel should yield to trowel, trowel to tweezers and whiskbroom if necessary. What good is it to find a rare ink bottle if you break it with your shovel?

Cleaning depends upon what you it is you find. Leather is one thing, wood is another. Many THers have taken one look at an icky green brass gizmo and thrown it back into the hole. Brass can be cleaned up, and the patina on a valuable piece adds rather than detracts to its value. The best advice is the get advice on how to clean a particular item. Usually a good detergent solution is helpful, but that is not always true. It could write

finis to a reclaimable item. Rust can be removed, paper preserved or even to some degree brought back, encrustations removed—and so on. Just get knowledgeable help and advice. If what you've found is worth anything, great, if it isn't, a little ridicule won't hurt you too much. Everyone thinks you're some kind of nut for THing, anyway.

Repair is just a more exacting repetition of what was just said. Go for help to someone who knows what they are doing. Again, books, old timers, and at time obvious specialists can often come up with exactly the suggestions or assistance you happen to need.

OLD TIMERS, AN OVERLOOKED RESEARCH AID

Talking to the old timers of an area in which a THer is interested is a must. If he truly wants to get first-rate information he cannot ignore what the older citizens of a given area have to say about it. Long time residents carry in their minds far more knowledge of dates, incidents, names, places, and mysterious going-ons than any other single source.

Talk with them! You can get more leads from this source than can be imagined. A few well directed questions can keep a conversation fom wandering. These folks like to talk, and far too often they are ignored. If they are approached right the elders of an area are usually pleased to share their knowledge and information with you.

Just remember who got you onto the lead, too, should it pan out. Too many older men and women in this land sit and wither away from indifference, poverty, and boredom. Should you recover a cache partially due to their aid, do what is right. That goes whether or not you have an agreement. It does not take a huge bundle of cash to vastly improve the economic condition most of these folks endure, and you will be rewarded multifold any cash involved.

Don't depend entirely upon your memory of any such conversations. Tape record them, if possible. If taping is not practical or possible for some reason, take notes, or write them up after the interview. You might take some pictures. People pass away, and you may have a very valuable resource. The facts stated by long-time residents of an area often fit like missing pieces of a jigsaw puzzle into old newspaper accounts, court records, and state or local historical accounts.

Ask for names and places, if they can tell you. Let them know your interest in robberies, misers, cases where supposedly wealthy people passed away and no money or other assets appeared, swindles, or local legends of buried treasure. Inquire about wealthy farmers whose heirs somehow didn't remain wealthy, especially if a once grand farmstead has now fallen into decay. This is just as true in towns.

If you ever become convinced a cache is located on a certain property, rent the property if it is possible to do so. If not, and your conviction is strong, you might consider buying the property. That usually is not necessary. Leasing, renting, making a search and salvage agreement, or offering a service of some sort could far more cheaply get the job done. If, however, you KNOW a good cache is in a certain place, purchase is not a bad way to go. It might turn into a good investment, for one thing, which is a different matter altogether.

One THer felt sure a farmer had cached money in a barn early in this century. After the farmer's death his heirs had sold the farm and moved away. Several different people had owned the farm in the intervening years. The THer went to the current owner and told him he wanted to tear down the old barn for its weathered lumber, for which in fact he did have a buyer. As the barn was not in good repair, and after considerable dickering, the farmer agreed to the THer's razing of the structure. The farmer wanted the THer to clean up any mess, of course. "Of course," agreed the THer. He made a pofit on the lumber, and he found a sizeable cache under the feed bins.

This particular recovery came, by the way, because that THer listened attentively to one sharp old-timer. No exact amount was divulged, but it was noticeable the old man's circumstances seemed better, and the THer had some brand new equipment.

This farmstead, north of Boulder, lies close by a locally legendary treasure supposed to be $80,000 in gold coins. $8,000 is more likely, but that still would be quite a find!

TAPING

There will be many times when a THer interviews people, that is if he is really interested in building up his lead file. It is perhaps the best way of getting reasonably accurate information about a given area. An interview with a long time resident cannot be beat for good leads.

In such interviews it is not always possible to take notes, and note taking very often bothers the person being interviewed. They get nervous. They clam up.

A good way around this problem is to have one of the multitude of good tape recorders on the market today. They are inexpensive, easy to use, and an interview can be taped entirely and accurately. Nothing is missed, and that is not always true with notetaking. Tones, pauses, important statements are caught down just as they were uttered. The tape can be rerun as many times as you want.

Go to one of the various outlets that handle tape recorders. It is an excellent method of adding to a lead file. You should get a unit that does not cost too much, and that you find easy to operate.

AERIAL PHOTOGRAPHY AND RECONNAISANCE

A great and largely unused tool for THers is the field of aerial photography. One does not have to be either a pilot nor a professional cameraman in order to use this versatile tool. Slower moving aircraft and helicopters have the most practical applications for the average THer, of course, for although more ground can be covered more quickly in high speed planes the high speed cameras required under such circumstances are beyond the financial means of most of us. Devices and techniques have continued to improve over the past few years. Highly accurate aerial photographs of excellent depth, color, and excellent quality are commonplace. If a THer needs this sort of help, and does not have the ability or equipment himself, the task can be done by a professional. The costs can be cheap, if one is looking for something in particular, for things have a way of showing up from the air that remain forever unseen at ground level.

A word of caution is in order. If photography assignments are given to somebody, that person should either not be told much if anything about what the searcher is looking for or else taken in on a split basis. This is just another good place where a blabbermouth can get edged out without ever realizing what is happening.

The Geodetic Survey was able to completely map the entire continental United States in a period of two years by using special aerial cameras. The ordinary THer is going to be concerned with a lot less area than that. Using surface techniques any area can be accurately mapped and photographed only by tedious and lengthy procedures. When one realizes that it would take about fifty years of plane table and level work to map the state of Pennsylvania alone, he can only be amazed at the speed and usefulness of aerial photography.

Take as many pictures as possible, from different altitudes and angles, and at early or late sunlight periods. Oblique sun rays highlight slight differences that pictures taken in middle daylight hours would never show. You may waste some film, but what you need also could show up on only one photograph out of hundreds.

Some reconnaissance prior to intensive photography is a good idea. A great deal of film and flying time may be saved. After all, just looking at an area from above very often gives the viewer a marvelous new viewpoint. At times what is being sought is seen, and landmarks observed that pinpoint the location. Even so, a ready camera will get in graphic form that which you saw. Eyesight can play tricks on a person, too, and a few pictures to carefully check in leisurely privacy can save a lot of fruitless hiking.

If you do see what you are flying around to see, cross the area at various angles and altitudes. This is important. Too much can be missed on only one or two passes. Things don't look the same from the ground, remember. Should you hurry back to the airport, leap in your vehicle, storm back as close as possible, and race to where you think it is, you may be disappointed. Hours or days or weeks of fruitless, tormenting search could force you skyward again when only a few more passes would have done it in the first place.

The author is no great shucks as a photographer, and is no plane or helicopter pilot at all. Nevertheless, from a THer's viewpoint, he can see the fantastic uses of aerial reconnaissance and photography. This brief treatment is to point out the possibilities to those who've not thought of using such techniques.

As a quick example, I flew over some old gold placer areas in Alaska in the summer of 1971. My brother is head mechanic for Merric Helicopter Service in Fairbanks and that summer they were ferrying work crews for several big mining firms far back into the boondocks each day from their base camp. An extensive mineral search is underway by the big firms all through the northlands, in case you are not aware of it. We were unable to get in much time, but in fifteen minutes we saw more than we could have explored afoot in days through that mosquito-ridden muskeg.

A very few THers have been doing this, with increasing success, for quite a few years. More have been discovering the value of such techniques.

Why not be selfish, and keep a good thing for myself? It is simple enough. The idea is ripe, for one thing, and not something all my own. The main thing, however, is that unless you have something in particular to look for, all you will get out of it is the fun of flying around. Remember that hideous word, RESEARCH? If you know something is in an area, and you can maintain silence and a poker face, you could fly over a certain spot, see it beyond any doubt, and even though you had a dozen companions, not a one of them would probably notice it. Why? You **knew what you were looking for.**

The same thing happens to the multitudes that beat to death our vanishing ghost towns. Casual tourists tramp around, blindly, destructively, and leave. Many a knowing THer has gone to such places, even with tourists nearby, and taken coins, artifacts, and even caches—for they knew what they were seeking.

So, should you have a need, look into the possibility of aerial photography and recconnaisance. Get a good pilot, who knows that particular area and all its potential hazards. If you need to, get a good professional photographer who has sophisticated enough equipment to meet your needs. If you have a good lead, grit your teeth and pay the bill, for it may be the key to a recovery.

Up we go, to seek afar on high the things below.

THE HELICOPTER

The helicopter offers a brand new horizon to THing. The "whirlybird" opens up a whole new set of opportunities to the thinking seeker of treasure. It all boils down to easier exploration and access to difficult areas.

First of all, that little flying machine can hover over any given spot, or cirle slowly. Pictures can be taken from different angles, at different times of the day. Spotting can be done that is much more difficult from even a small plane, as effective as that can be. Equipment can be brought in and landed in places burros, let alone four-wheel-drive vehicles, could not go, and efficient base camps set up. The helicopter need not stay, but can return at given times.

The use of such a machine is not cheap, or at least not at first glance. It is if your time and effort are worth anything. A helicopter could be the least expensive part of a search for something really valuable. If you really believe your lead to be good the helicopter could speed up your search and exploration tremendously. Mapping and pictures could be far more rapidly and accurately completed, plus an excellent overall picture of the area formed. Things can be seen from the air that simply are not noticed down at ground level. The establishment of a base camp at previously unfeasible sites is no small consideration.

If you have something going for you, consider the use of a helicopter. Find out if one is available in your area. It could be well worth its cost. It could save days, weeks, or even months of frustrating search on foot, and such frustration has caused many a person to give up good leads.

A new book, HUNTING LOST MINES BY HELICOPTER, is now available. It may prove quite helpful to some!

FOUR-WHEEL DRIVE VEHICLES

The author does not come close to being an expert on this particular subject, being no four-wheeled-drive-buff. Even so, he is very familiar indeed with the greater ease and quickness a great many out-of-the-way spots can be reached by using such vehicles. To put a long story in a few words, these motorized mules save a lot of walking and lugging.

Anyone really intending to do a lot of back-country exploration should probably consider the purchase of such an aid. I would advise careful consideration and comparison as to price, use, longevity and durability of the machine. A wise purchase should last for a good many years, barring accident and foolishness.

A four-wheel-drive is not a magic carpet. It may go where the roads get bad, or even at times where there are no roads at all, but that can lead the unwary THer to troubles undreamed of. No long list is required, but a few will probably be sufficient to warn the unwary.

Get all four wheels off the ground, propped up on a high center, and it can be a real chore getting off. Get mired down in muck up over the akles, and that can be even worse. A good winch in such a case helps, but it is best if you only get stuck where a nice tree is close by. Ever try to winch out where there is nothing to anchor to? Fun! Go across a deep gully, just before a heavy rainstorm, into the backlands via that one-and-only "road". It is a good way to get an extended vacation. Forget a can or two of extra gasoline. Don't check the water in your battery or radiator. Attempt to turn around on a soft-shouldered shelf road.

That brief list should be ample.

Even so, there is nothing like a good four-wheeled-drive to cut hours and labor for a THer who often heads for the far back.

HIKING

When it comes right down to it, the best way of getting to where you want to go is by hiking. One foot in front of the other. The Ther unwilling or unable to walk a good deal is going to have a great lmitation placed on his hunting.

Four-wheeled-drive vehicles are great for getting back into tough areas far off the paved roads. Motor bikes undoubtedly extend that help, and many THers profit by their use. Even so, there is going to be a great deal of old-fashioned hoofing it if a really thorough job is to be done.

Today's seeker of treasure should definitely keep one thing in mind, and that is the ecology/conservation emotion currently sweeping the country. Heedless and thoughtless four-wheelers or hikers, who really are a small minority, make it tough on their fellow enthusiasts, many of whom are THers. Areas that have been in the past open to such activities have either already been closed to wheeled traffic or stringently limited. Once again the pleasure of many careful, thoughful people is wiped out by the actions of a few don't-give-a-damners.

A horse can be ridden into such areas, and such a method is perhaps the very best way in certain instances, but for many THers the elimination of wheeled vehicles means either hiking in or forgetting certain locations. After all, there's a good many people in this country these days who don't know how to get on a horse, let alone staying on one once they get there. We won't even mention the problem of navigation. Thus, applied shoe leather.

Walking is a good sport, and it is undoubtedly the only real way to properly explore a given area carefully. There have been various articles concerning the thrills of going THing, bottle hunting, or gem stone hunting from a bike, or from a four-wheeler. Pardon my raised eyebrows, but such activity is more the fun of vehicle operation than it is THing. Such vehicles are excellent for aiding access to good aeas, but once there the footwork becomes imperative.

The tired muscles one gets from such activity do not go unrewarded, not even though nothing of great monetary value is gained on a trip. An overview of an area gained afoot is amazing. There is enough time to appreciate what one sees along the way. Also, those sore muscles indicate their use, and use of muscles makes for a better, healthier body. Healthy bodies last longer, which means even more THing trips. How can a person beat that?

MAPPING

People forget things. They think they will remember, but things are easily forgotten under the best of circumstances. Under the lash of excitement memoy tends to be downright foggy. Some people have made a great deal of fun over the "lost ledges", the "lost mines", and the "rich placers once found and never relocated". The truth of the matter is that there really have been a good many such instances. The reason for such stories is simple. People forget things, and excitement or hurriedness makes forgetting even easier.

Which brings up the necessity of making a map when actively THing. As a person woks an area it behooves him to keep a map, rough or polished according to his abilities, indicating his work. Then, should he discover anything of value, it can be noted with ample references to surroundings.

This procedure is not difficult. It can be done on a USGS or any good topographical map. Such maps are available for most areas across the United States. Whether looking for placer depositis, caches, old house sites, or anything; a simple mapping procedure can easily be followed. It could save the THer much heartbreak and futility, too.

MAPPING AND THE USE OF MAPS IN TREASURE HUNTING

The use of maps in THing can be vitally important to consistently successful recovery. By maps, I do not mean the crude type on supposedly old paper or parchment that is alleged to lead directly to where someone buried untold wealth. If a person really believed he had a true map of that sort he would not be trying to sell it, he would be out searching. The maps important to the THer of today are road maps, atlases, county maps, USGS topographical sheets, maps of the same area drawn at different dates over a long period of time, maps one creates in his own search and research, and of course if a crude map of authentic origin turns up, then a crude old map.

A map is a means of seeing broad spatial relationships. Man is too close to the world he lives on to really see it. He needs to bring things down to a size more his own, something he can visualize and think about. A map puts things into a manageable perspective. The map is a research tool too seldom used. A person can quickly put together entirely different perspectives of an area when he begins to get isolated facts concerning that area down on a map.

A case in point: In certain areas old coins have been found by different people. A bit of research will often allow one to map the findings on say a county or city map, and it is amazing how the probable source of those coins begins to narrow. It is the author's belief that such a technique would be most beneficial at certain sites along beaches where treasure laden ships were broken up. Actual recoveries have been made with such mapping techniques, and one would have been speeded by years if such a system had been used. Hit or miss searching simply takes too long.

THE VALUE OF OLD COINS

Inflation is a word most of us understand only too well in this hard-to-keep-up-let-alone-get-ahead world. It simply means that what we save, if we save anything, is eroded away by a shrinking dollar's buying power. Only through INVESTMENT, and wise investment, can a person hope to see their savings actually grow instead of shrinking in value. Too many people neither understand, have the capital, or have the contacts required to invest wisely and well in the stock market, art, real estate, or other such things. When sch people get into such speculation, in spite of their ignorance and inability, they most often get hurt. The stock that looked as though it might go up went down. The property was good, but was already appreciated, or needed repair, or was too far away from the center of town, or too close in to the center of town, or a thousand other reasons. The art work did have a real artist behind it: a con artist. You have heard such stories of people trying to fight inflation and losing.

What is most disheartening is that by giving up and not fighting, like a wasting sickness, is also losing. A long, dreary losing.

THers have a splendid way of really fighting inflation. Some of those coins the avid THer comes up with are worth real money now and are bound to be worth even more in the future. A coin that the ecstatic treasure hunter finds is worth $250 on the numismatic market may sell it, blow the cash, and find in ten years that he could have made 25%, 50% or even more, **each year for ten years.** It has been done. It will continue to be done. If a guy does not need to sell the coin he should not—he should set it aside as a wise investment.

Think about the opportunity you have. First, you FOUND the coin. You had the pleasure of finding it. You had gotten along without it before you found it, so if you really don't need the cash its sale would bring, why sell it? It has a definite personal meaning to you, for you can show it to interested friends and acquaintances, and it will always be an interesting conversation piece. If it is now valuable there is little chance it will become less valuable as long as the inflationary trend continues. There is a remarkable probability that it will become increasingly valuable with each passing year. All this on the investment of primarily time, which you probably enjoyed investing and would have spent looking whether you found a valuable coin or not.

Therefore, why not turn such an item into a sound, long-term investment, and one to which there will constantly be possible additions? Numismatics is a field with which most THers should acquaint and associate themselves with.

You do not have to become an avid collector. You can be a collector/investor. There are many such people these days, folks who have realized that the hobby can be a growth investment with potential capital expansion not available to them elsewhere. They know that as increasing interest in numismatics, and in investments in numismatics grow, they cannot help but profit. Increased interest means increased demand, and there are a very limited number of the really good coins.

Some of the coins you find, of course, will not be the really good ones. Many will be worn, tarnished, or damaged. You probably will damage a few yourself in getting them from their hidey-hole, no matter how careful you may be. Should these be saved?

The Good Book says that a wise man sold all he had and bought a pearl of great price. This is pertinent to THers and any or all of the worn, common-date, damaged, tarnished, or otherwise doubtful coins you come across. It is not bad advice to say, save your silver coins of such caliber until you have enough to purchase ONE **good** coin, and buy it. Buy it from a coin shop, and get the best possible price for your silver coins. I might say the same for other coins, too, for it is far, far more potentially profitable to have ONE twenty dollar, uncirculated or proof coin than it is for you to squirrel away 2000 wheat-ear, common-date, corroded pennies. Consider carefully, and you will realize that ten years from now, those pennies maybe, and I stress the maybe, will bring you $20.00 or $40.00. That uncrculated coin very well may go up 15%, 20%, or more a year during those ten years, and end up being worth several times what the pennies would bring. That plus the fact that one coin could be sold far more easily and quickly than the 2000 poor quality pennies.

Definitely consider proof sets. In 1972 the 1936 proof set has been selling for over $800. That is an over 2400% gain. And it has sold for as high as $1000 per set, and should do so again. That is over 80% per year for anyone who bought a set in 1936 and sold it this year. Interesting? I cannot help but think so.

Any of those proof sets are good investments, and well worth trading for common coins you've found. Individual proof coins and uncirculated coins are equally interesting and potentially profitable. Be cautioned, however, to choose wisely.

Go to a reputable coin dealer. Join a coin club. Talk, listen, and when you invest, do if only after deliberation. It will add new and intruiging dimensions to your THing. Such interest on your part will create an investment possibility on your part that you may heretofore never have dreamed of.

IMPROVING OUR HOBBY'S STATUS

THing is no longer a matter of just getting out and enjoying a marvelous hobby. Too bad, but that is the way it is. These days most people recognize a THer for what he is. There was a time not too very long ago that seekers of treasure posed as eccentrics, servicemen, scientists, and all sorts of things, to conceal their actual objective. The general public is more aware of the field now, and a ruse has to really be exceptional if one wished to cover their actual motives. It can be and is being done, but to do so becomes increasingly difficult.

These days the THing field is in somewhat the same boat as big game hunters. The actions of a few inconsiderates and slobs give a bad name to everyone in the field. If we wish to enjoy a growing hobby field it is up to all of us to police our own ranks and discipline our own activities. When we see some geezer digging holes we should tell him about it. If some joker is tearing into old buildings it is our business. One doesn't have to take the law into their own hands, but he should know that someone is willing to have the law take the law, and him, into their own hands. Tearing into old buildings is completely ridiculous, and good THers pride themselves upon leaving a place looking just like they found it.

We all have to realize that we do create an impression as a group, be it good or bad. Yes, it is still best to remain quietly out of sight, if it is possible, but it is not possible for most. Therefore it falls upon each of us to act as builders of good will. That is not a hard thing to do. Courteous actions, the wonderful, not-out-of-date golden rule, and ordinary common (which really is not common at all) sense will work wonders and open gates to THers most of the time. It will help other THers, too, people they may never even meet.

The author and Jerry McCarty (author of Louisiana-Mississippi treasure leads) locating a pot full of rich barnyard beneath the doorstep of a Kansas shed.

THE PAST, THE PRESENT, AND THE FUTURE OF THing

Treasure hunting is not new. People have hunted for coins since coins first became a medium of exchange. Many individuals probably edged themselves a shaky step out of grinding poverty by carefully looking over the picnic and party areas where wealthier citizens of their time frolicked. The Spanish search for gold throughout the Americas, to a great degree, was a tremendous treasure hunt. In this century more and more men and a few women became aware of the fantastic, unrecovered treasures and the opportunities for sudden wealth unrecognized by the multitudes. Some of these folks made large and small fortunes, even before metal detectors made the process simpler, simply by **good research,** keeping eyes and ears open, thinking out each situation, and working diligently at what they were doing.

The treasure hunting of a few years ago was a glorious thing. There was really not much competition for a hard-working, analytical THer. The sky was the limit, and the rewards often proved astonishing. Karl von Mueller tells me, as he will in his own frank way anyone else, that such days are over. I agree with him.

Today there is increasing competition. Many "THers" are really hobbiests (which I think is great!). Laws, bureaucratic decrees and harrassments, and sheer people pressure tend to make many areas increasingly difficult to hunt. Not impossible, just more difficult. Some fantastic recoveries have been made, some reported, many completely unreported.

THing today is not what it used to be. It has changed. This is no reason to give up, though, for I think the potential rewards are as great as they ever were, perhaps more so. Not for everybody, they aren't, for the challenge is greater, the task more difficult. A THer, to be successful, must continually research, use his head to go where he needs to go, keep an ever-tighter closed mouth, and keep up on the technological improvements.

Metal detectors have definitely improved, these past few years. The competition among manufacturing firms is fierce, and I think this is a good thing. There have been improvements. There promises to be more, and all this must make for better detectors. Look closely at the new machines. Demand hard demonstrations. Ask embarrassing questions.

Don't buy on impulse, and know your dealer. There are so many, many fine people in this field—don't get products from someone who only sells detectors, get them from those who will and can help you, who will back up their products.

More money is being lost today than ever before. More money is being squirrelled away, too, for about the same reasons as people had in the past. This in spite of the banks—perhaps partially because of them. The people of this nation have money. Kids lose small fortunes, right out of their careless, grubby little hands and pockets. After all, the folks will give them more.

So don't give up. THing is alive and well, and the future reaches out before us. Surely dangers threaten the hobby. We all are threatened by this or that from the day we are born, on. Maybe there are too many THers, but I doubt it. The lazy, thoughtless, or rather indifferent ones will not adversely affect us for long, for they will soon give up. Those who remain active of mind and body in this field will do well, even if it is only to add years of zestful living. Is that not a treasure in itself, not to be purchased with full casks of jewels?

The future of THing? Who knows, exactly, but I, for one, intend to enjoy it!

A cache such as this one, found in Minnesota, is what THing is all about. There were several coins in this lot well worth setting aside as a long term investment.

Unique, weathered fenceposts such as this can bring a premium price on the landscaping/decor market. Such posts can often be purchased from farmers after the bases rot out and they are replaced by new posts.

Indians once camped on this small rise above Left Hand Canyon. The oldest cabin in Boulder County stood until recently just this side of the cottonwoods. Now a golf course adjoins the site to the east. This is the way one culture, one land-use after another often comes in succession

CONCLUSION

The tale goes on. As paths never really end, wandering as they do, on away from what you thought was your destination, the adventure of treasure hunting never really ends, either. The search continues, the adventure of never knowing what you will find goes on, and THing becomes more of a way of life than a mere hobby. This book may end, and I hope it is of interest and help to those who read it, but those who are real THers will go on with their own adventures and live a good many intriguing chapters of their own.

This was not written to be only an armchair THer's evening reading. I hope it will serve as a spur to many, and encourage them in their own, personal search for treasure, whatever or wherever it may be. Perhaps we shall meet, afield somewhere—whether or no, the best of luck!

H. Glenn Carson

Other books available from True Treasure Library —

- DIRECTORY OF BURIED OR SUNKEN TREASURES AND LOST MINES OF THE UNITED STATES
- TREASURE GUIDE TO NEBRASKA — KANSAS — NORTH DAKOTA — SOUTH DAKOTA
- A GUIDE TO TREASURE IN CALIFORNIA
- A GUIDE TO TREASURE IN TEXAS
- A GUIDE TO TREASURE IN ARKANSAS — LOUISIANA — MISSISSIPPI
- A GUIDE TO TREASURE IN ARIZONA
- A GUIDE TO TREASURE IN NEVADA
- A GUIDE TO TREASURE IN NEW MEXICO
- A GUIDE TO TREASURE IN MISOURI
- A GUIDE TO TREASURE IN UTAH
- A GUIDE TO TREASURE IN MONTANA AND WYOMING
- A GUIDE TO TREASURE IN ILLINOIS AND INDIANA
- A GUIDE TO TREASURE IN MICHIGAN AND OHIO
- A GUIDE TO TREASURE IN PENNSYLVANIA
- A GUIDE TO TREASURE IN VIRGINIA AND WEST VIRGINIA
- A GUIDE TO TREASURE IN KENTUCKY

FREE Treasure Reference Catalog.   **Dealer Discounts available.**